GOD REST YE MERRY, SOLDIERS

A True Civil War
Christmas Story

James McIvor

A PLUME BOOK

PLUME
Published by Penguin Group
Penguin Group (USA) Inc., 375 Hudson Street, New York, New York 10014, U.S.A.
Penguin Group (Canada), 90 Eglinton Avenue East, Suite 700, Toronto, Ontario, Canada
M4P 2Y3 (a division of Pearson Penguin Canada Inc.)
Penguin Books Ltd., 80 Strand, London WC2R 0RL, England
Penguin Ireland, 25 St. Stephen's Green, Dublin 2, Ireland (a division of Penguin Books Ltd.)
Penguin Group (Australia), 250 Camberwell Road, Camberwell, Victoria 3124, Australia (a divi-
sion of Pearson Australia Group Pty. Ltd.)
Penguin Books India Pvt. Ltd., 11 Community Centre, Panchsheel Park, New Delhi – 110
017, India
Penguin Books (NZ), cnr Airborne and Rosedale Roads, Albany, Auckland 1310, New
Zealand (a division of Pearson New Zealand Ltd.)
Penguin Books (South Africa) (Pty.) Ltd., 24 Sturdee Avenue, Rosebank, Johannesburg 2196,
South Africa

Penguin Books Ltd., Registered Offices: 80 Strand, London WC2R 0RL, England

Published by Plume, a member of Penguin Group (USA) Inc. Previously published in a
Viking edition.

First Plume Printing, November 2006
10 9 8 7 6 5 4 3 2 1

℗ REGISTERED TRADEMARK—MARCA REGISTRADA

LIBRARY OF CONGRESS CATALOGING-IN-PUBLICATION DATA

McIvor, James.
    God rest ye merry, soldiers : a Civil War Christmas story / James McIvor.
        p. cm.
    Includes bibliographical references.
    ISBN 0-670-03451-7 (hc.)
    ISBN 0-452-28769-3 (pbk.)
    1. Soldiers—United States—Social life and customs—19th century. 2. Soldiers—Confederate
States of America—Social life and customs. 3. Christmas—United States—History—19th
century. 4. Christmas—Southern States—History—19th century. 5. United States.
Army—Military life—
History—19th century. 6. Confederate States of America. Army—Military life. 7. United
States—History—Civil War, 1861–1865—Social aspects. I. Title.
    E607.M33 2005
    973.7'8—dc22   2005042202

Printed in the United States of America
Original hardcover design by Carla Bolte

A PLUME BOOK

GOD REST YE MERRY, SOLDIERS

JAMES MCIVOR is a longtime Civil War enthusiast and freelance writer who lives in Virginia.

"[A] charming stocking stuffer . . . distinctly readable and moving throughout."　　　—*Publishers Weekly*

"McIvor's slim, simple little book about . . . the experience of Christmas during and after the war benefits from the equal amount of empathy he grants to both Yankee and Confederate soldiers, far from home at the loneliest time of the year."　　　—*Entertainment Weekly*

"McIvor writes with precision and grace and has unearthed a lode of Civil War–era Christmas poems and songs that general readers will enjoy. He has also mined a cache of original letters and diary entries that convey the pathos and tragedy of war without romanticizing the complexities, frustrations, and ambivalent feelings. . . . McIvor's little book underscores the meaning of Christmas for nations at war, when memories of home and longings for the safe return of loved ones preoccupy families rich and poor."　　　—*BookPage*

CONTENTS

God Rest Ye Merry, Soldiers

1

CHRISTMAS 1862

On Christmas Day 1862, North Carolina soldier Constantine A. Hege wrote his parents, full of the homesickness and weariness that gripped many a soldier that second Christmas of war.

"Christmas has come once more and it is a very beautiful morning," Hege began, "but O! how changed the scene to what it was last Christmas. To day twelve months ago I was home where I could enjoy the blessings of a comfortable house and home of parents and friends and of religious worship, but this Christmas I am surrounded by warriors, cannons, and guns. . . . But I hope and pray that the good Lord in his tender mercy may soon bring this state of things to an end and restore Peace and prosperity to our

1

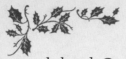

beloved Country again and turn the hearts of the rulers to peace for ever instead of war."

A year before, Christmas in army camps and at hearth sides North and South had been alive with high spirits. In 1861, war was still a romantic adventure, a chance for dashing feats and excitement. Soldiers had gone off to war that first year as if heading for a "frolic," said one civilian who watched them go. Both sides were sure of quick and glorious victory. An Alabama soldier confidently predicted in 1861 that peace would surely come in 1862 because there simply wouldn't be any Yankee soldiers left alive once the Southern boys had had a crack at them. "I think I can whip 25 myself," he boasted. Northerners were just as confident that the ragtag rebels would be crushed in short order, and the Union restored.

That first year, camp life was still a novelty and an adventure for men who had never before ventured far from home. Many a soldier's letter described a Christmas Day of 1861 full of camaraderie and high jinks, brass bands and sports, good food and drink. Soldiers chased greased pigs and ran footraces. Some staged mock parades, banging on tin pans as they marched through camp. Officers and privates alike put together

elaborate Christmas feasts of turkey, mince pies, cakes, eggnog, and whiskey. Food was still plentiful at homes and farms as yet untouched by the sting of war, and a popular treat for soldiers in camp was a gift box, shipped by express, from loved ones at home. *Harper's Weekly* had depicted that first wartime Christmas with a cover illustration showing soldiers merrily opening boxes sent from parents or sisters. The most popular items from home were whiskey, hams, cooked chickens, cakes, socks, boots, and warm clothes.

The Christmas illustration in *Harper's* a year later captured the far more somber mood that now gripped the nation. "The happy few may, perhaps, again this year celebrate their annual festivities," the magazine allowed, "but oh! to how many will it be a season of sad, sad memories!" The accompanying illustration, by the famous *Harper's* artist Thomas Nast, showed a young wife kneeling by the bedside of her two sleeping babies, gazing out the window at the moon over a snow-covered landscape as she clasps to her breast a small framed portrait. Opposite this scene of home, her soldier husband is shown sitting by a lonely campfire, gun in one hand, and he too holds a framed portrait of his loved ones as the moon shines down over

a frozen river. The third prominent element of the illustration is a vignette of soldiers' graves.

Where a year before soldiers had written home full of patriotic zeal and brash confidence of victory, now many openly prayed that the war would just be over and that they might be home with their families again.

"Another Christmas is past and gone!" wrote Confederate captain Jim Womack of the 16th Tennessee Infantry. "How differently spent from that of '61! That I passed in Charleston and Fort Sumter, where I was delighted and pleased; this I have spent in my tent by the fire near Murfreesboro, attending to many of the daily duties of the soldier. May the coming Christmas in '63 find our now distracted and unhappy country reposing in the lap of an infantile and glorious peace."

❧⟶❦

For many, the Christmas of '62 afforded not even a brief respite from the grim press, or just plain tedium, of war. President and Mrs. Lincoln spent part of the day visiting the men who now crowded hospitals in the capital, wounded in the recent fighting at Antietam

4

in nearby Maryland—where, in a single, terrible day, six thousand had died and seventeen thousand were wounded.

William M. Woodcock, a Union soldier in the 9th Kentucky Infantry, jotted down in his diary the abortive attempt of the men in his regiment to get a celebration going on this Christmas Day: "All hands raised hollering 'Christmas Gift,' 'Hurrah for Christmas,' etc. but were soon stopped in their preparations for a gala day by an order to get ready immediately to go on picket." An Ohio soldier stationed north of Murfreesboro, Tennessee, wrote simply, "Christmas day was no holiday for us. After breakfast we received orders to march."

Elias D. Moore of the 114th Ohio Volunteer Infantry spent Christmas on a gunboat that had been sent down the Mississippi to the Yazoo River. The day turned out to be just any other day of army hurry-up-and-wait drill and bad army food. "We awoke this morning by being called to go on guard," Moore wrote in his diary on Christmas Day 1862. "At noon I eat my Christmas dinner off a cracker. Fat meat and coffee made of water caught out of the boiler and was not boilt."

Many soldiers' thoughts on Christmas Day of 1862 turned to the familiar comforts of holiday food of celebrations gone by. But absent this year was the abundance of family feasts of years past; gone were even the improvised Christmas meals that soldiers had managed to put together the year before with gifts from home. Wartime shortages were beginning to tell. In Richmond, turkeys were going for eleven dollars each, sugar for candies and cakes was eight dollars a pound. There were far fewer delicacies in the express boxes this year. The sutlers who peddled their wares to soldiers in camp were charging outrageous prices for the few treats they had to offer: a dollar a pound for butter, fifty cents a pound for some dubious sausages. "Christmas has come and gone," wrote Reuben Searcy of the 34th Alabama to his mother from camp near Murfreesboro, Tennessee, on the day after Christmas. "But how differently did I celebrate its coming this year. The only thing that impressed me with the fact that it was Christmas was that we did not have drill, and a drink of some fourteen-year-old whiskey that was given to me by a friend."

One Southern lady tried to make light of the hardships and shortages with a humorous poem that was printed in the December 1862 edition of the *Southern Illustrated News*. Santa Claus, she explained, had simply fallen afoul of the Yankee blockade:

> *This happened one Christmas. I'm sorry to write,*
> *Our ports are blockaded, and Santa, to-night,*
> *Will hardly get down here; for if he should start,*
> *The Yankees would get him unless he was "smart."*
> *They beat all the men in creation to run*
> *And if they could get him, they'd think it fine fun*
> *To put him in prison, and steal the nice toys*
> *He started to bring to our girls and boys.*
> *But try not to mind it—tell over your jokes—*
> *Be gay and be cheerful, like other good folks;*
> *For if you remember to be good and kind,*
> *Old Santa next Christmas will bear it in mind.*

But the truth was that for many it was the bleakest Christmas in many a year. "Christmas Day, the poorest ever spent," recorded a Virginia soldier, "no eggnog, no turkey, no mince pie, nothing to eat or drink but our rations. We all talk of home today and wish to be there." Outside of Fredericksburg, Virginia, Major Frederick L. Hitchcock of the 132nd Pennsylvania

Volunteers recorded in his diary his meager Christmas dinner: hardtack soaked in water, then fried in pork fat. "The wish for a 'Merry Christmas' was about all there was to make it such," he added glumly.

Colonel Charles D. Haydon of the 2nd Michigan described his even less appetizing meal: "We made Christmas dinner on beef, hard tack & coffee. I had fortunately completed my meal when Moore made a discovery which checked him midway in his, viz that the hard tacks were full of bugs & worms. This is no uncommon thing of late, but his wry face was the most laughable thing of the day."

∙∙∙

Some Southern regiments, especially, resorted to drowning their sorrows in whatever whiskey they could still scrounge up and to distracting themselves with rough practical jokes of their own making. One young member of a Confederate unit was sent by his comrades with a dollar to buy what he could in the way of food and drink. He came back with ninety cents' worth of whiskey and ten cents' of bread. His colleagues upbraided him severely for having been so simpleminded as to spend so much on bread. The

officers of the 20th Tennessee Infantry managed to procure a barrel of whiskey for their men to celebrate a merry Christmas, but the result was more violent than merry. "We had many a drunken fight and knock-down before the day was closed," recorded one soldier.

The 45th Tennessee Infantry, encamped at Murfreesboro, was better off than many of its fellow Confederate units since its members had been largely recruited from the immediate vicinity. The farms of Middle Tennessee had yet to suffer the depredations of war and blockade that had already beset much of the South, and many of the 45th had been given furloughs to visit their homes. They came back with home-baked pies and cakes.

But in the air of gloom and scarcity that filled the camp, the sudden appearance of these Christmas delicacies evoked more jealousy and hard feelings than goodwill toward men. The soldiers of the 20th Tennessee, who were not so fortunate, promptly hatched a plan to seize by force and subterfuge some of the 45th's windfall. A snowball fight was arranged between the two regiments. As one member of the 20th recounted, "A charge was ordered and the boys of the

20th mixed up with the 45th in their own camp and the battle waxed warm; and while about three-fourths of the 20th were waging war in the heart of the 45th's camp, the other one-fourth was packing off into our camp whatever they could. When the fight was over the 45th did not have near as many good things as they did when it opened; they even lost a large percent of their cooking utensils, and the best of their arms.

"In the thickest of the fight two large soldiers caught me and I was thrown into a ditch; one of them held me while the other nearly smothered me with snow, but I was doing my best to entertain them for I knew that some of our men were confiscating what they had."

Even the few traditional Christmas delicacies the soldiers could lay their hands on this Christmas had a way of turning to ashes in their mouths. What had, the year before, been a re-creation of the comforts of Christmas at home was now a mocking reminder of how utterly impossible it was for Christmas in an army camp to be anything like Christmas at home. "At the expense of one dollar and seventy-five cents, I procured a small turkey and had a Christmas dinner," wrote Union soldier John Beatty, "but it lacked the collaterals, and was a failure." Reuben Jones of the 19th U.S. Regulars received a Christmas box with a pound cake that his cousin Ann had baked, but what he appreciated far more was the practical gift of a pair of gloves from his brother. "Those gloves bless your soul give me more comfort on the battlefield than $10,000 would have," he wrote a couple of weeks after Christmas. "I slept in them I have worn them out already."

Homesickness, and the contrast between this Christmas and Christmases past, was the theme that this year filled the hearts and minds of the more reflective men, of North and South alike. "Today is Christmas eve Tomorrow is Christmas agin & here we are around our camp fire again instead of being at home enjoying ourselves with the ones we love best as we were want in days gone by to spend the Merry Christmas Holy days," wrote a Virginia soldier who had not seen his wife and children for sixteen months. "Oh how much happier I would feel today were I with you to spend the Christmastide even if I could stay but a short time." He added that for some men of the company the desire to be at home this time of year had proved too great: "5 of our company deserted a few nights ago & went home to spend the Christmas."

Adding to homesickness this season was real sickness, and—for the Union troops encamped around Nashville and the Confederates at Murfreesboro—the knowledge that they would soon be engaged in a major battle.

Sickness hit particularly hard among the farm boys from the old Northwest who filled the Union regiments fighting in Tennessee, Kentucky, and other states west of the Appalachians. They had not been exposed to the childhood diseases that city-dwelling boys had contracted, and developed an immunity to, in infancy. And so in the crowded camps, with their often less than sanitary conditions, they dropped like flies. "This is Christmas, and what a contrast between our Christmas and those who are home in good, comfortable houses, with plenty to eat and good beds to sleep in, and good nurses when sick," lamented John Chilcote of the 19th Ohio Infantry from camp outside Nashville. "The measles, mumps, chicken pox, small pox and about everything else has broken loose and taken hold of the boys."

The 19th Ohio's colonel recorded the scene in camp that night as the men tried to get a celebration going that quickly gave way to their true feelings. "The men

gathered about the camp fires during the evening hours with abortive attempts at merriment, soon to be given up, and then to talk in whispers of friends and family and home. The bugle calls, holding out the promise that balmy sleep might bring forgetfulness, were welcomed; although tattoo seemed a wail, and lights-out a sob."

Nearby, two brothers in the 21st Ohio Volunteer Infantry, Alfred and Addison Searles, sat down to write their father on Christmas Day. "They have commenced a fight in hearing of us, what or how much we don't know," the brothers wrote. "They are cannoning for keeps by the sound for the past 1/2 hour. It may be a general engagement and it may not, but I cannot say. The Boys are not in very good spirits, for this is Christmas Day, the second time and a good prospect for the 3rd now, and they are all past and cannot help themselves but this is a deadener upon this country."

Sitting by himself by the fire in the camp of the Pioneer Battalion near Nashville that night, Henry V. Freeman of the 74th Illinois Volunteer Infantry was also in a reflective mood. "Last night was Christmas Eve," he wrote in his first entry in the small pocket

memorandum book that he later "sent home in lieu of a letter" to his family. "It brought to my mind a thousand recollections of the past. The contrast is great. I sat up late in the evening at the fire, after attending to drawing rations, for we were under marching orders for this morning at five o'clock. About eleven o'clock at night heard heavy firing in front. Where will the next Christmas Eve find me?"

Years later Freeman wrote somewhat ruefully that "perhaps the touch of sentiment" from "the rather forlorn individual who made that entry, sitting alone that Christmas Eve beside his camp-fire, after his comrades had retired to sleep . . . may be forgiven in a boy who, nineteen years of age, had left his home only the September before, entering the army at the time when he had intended to enter upon his college course, an intention not to be realized until after three years of a soldier's life."

⋈⋈

Part of what made the contrast of Christmas at home so great for these men was the way Christmas in America had begun, of late, to be the special holiday

14

it would be for generations ever after—a holiday of family and home.

It hadn't always been that way. In the early years of America the Puritans had sternly disapproved of any Christmas revelry. The Massachusetts Puritan divine Cotton Mather preached from his Boston pulpit in 1712 condemning those who would "turn the grace of God into wantonness" with their Christmas celebrations. The Puritans pointed out that there was no scriptural authority for placing Christ's birth in December; the early Church had done so merely in an attempt to Christianize the pagan winter solstice holidays that were a feature of most traditional agricultural societies. But the Church paid a heavy price in so doing. The pagan revelries were holidays traditionally marked by excess, public carryings-on, and a kind of officially sanctioned lawlessness in which roving bands of merrymakers would forcibly enter landowners' homes demanding food and drink—and threatening acts of vandalism if they were not satisfied, in a sort of adult version of trick-or-treat. And so Christmas in the Old World had taken on many of these same traditions. But what did such unbiblical

"superstition and excess" have to do with the birth of the Savior, the New England Puritans demanded? To stamp out such impiety, they ordained that December 25 would be a workday like any other.

In the antebellum South, by contrast, Christmas had long been marked by excesses that seemed to fully justify the Puritans' abhorrence. The holiday was much more a licentious public carnival than a religious, or even a family, observance. Bands of fantastically arrayed riders would go from plantation to plantation, engaging in clownish behavior. Guns would be fired off to greet the holiday. Days or even weeks of balls and parties and "idleness" and "lounging" and "dissipation" marked the Christmas season. As many a visitor remarked, drink flowed with an abundance that routinely reached the point of wretched excess. One Southern lady recorded in her diary that the first thing she did on Christmas morning was to have "a joyful eggnog drink—I really got tight." And one plantation visitor wrote, "Sudden calls for the doctor to attend cases of delirium tremens were numerous during Christmas."

But in both North and South, the decades leading up to the war had seen a mellowing of attitudes and

a new warmth and softness to Christmas—more open-hearted in Puritan New England, more domestic in the old South. Magazines and books began to enthusiastically embrace and promote the "traditional German Christmas," with its emphasis on family and home, its nostalgic traditions binding the generations together. *Harper's* and *Godey's Lady's Book* popularized the Christmas tree with stories and illustrations. At Christmastime, magazine pages were now filled with sentimental poems and stories and recipes for mince pie and plum pudding and other traditional favorites. The image of Santa Claus had appeared in a Philadelphia store window in 1841 and soon became a staple of the American Christmas. By 1856, the poet Henry Wadsworth Longfellow could write that Christmas in New England was in a "transition stage; the old puritan feeling prevents it from being a cheerful, hearty holiday; though every year makes it more so."

By the time of the Civil War, nearly all the states of the country had made Christmas a legal holiday; even Puritan Massachusetts, which had once ordered its courts to remain open on December 25, now closed all public offices and forbade commercial transactions on Christmas Day. It had become a day to set aside the

toils of work and to spend quietly at home with one's family.

Above all, this new Christmas that was slowly taking root in America was a holiday of, and for, children. It was a time not just to bring joy to children with surprise gifts of toys and candies; it was a time to celebrate the innocence of childhood itself and the sheltering morality of home and family against a troubled world. A popularizer of this new, more innocent, more sentimental holiday invoked the purity of childhood that the spirit of Christmas celebrated: "Let the graces of childhood elevate our souls, and purify us of all contamination of anger and wrath. . . . Oh that we might all be like unto our children, to whom the invisible love of God is made manifest in the Christchild under the form of an innocent babe, like unto them in appearance, but descending from heaven with pleasant gifts." In celebrating Christmas by bringing simple joy to children, we could celebrate the purity and goodness of the child that remained in all of us, still uncorrupted by the sins of the world.

❧❀❦

And so the soldiers who huddled about campfires in the trenches before Fredericksburg, or along the desolate shores of the Yazoo River, or outside of Nashville or Murfreesboro bracing for the battle whose first rumbles could already be heard, felt a nostalgic longing that went beyond a want of mince pies and eggnog. "'A merry Christmas,' said I to myself, for want of a larger family-circle," lamented one soldier in a letter to his mother on Christmas morning. A few days later he mused to himself, "Family ties are never so close as in these days of separation and trial."

There had been something undeniably childlike about the soldiers who had first gone off to war, so full of boyish enthusiasm and a sense of adventure. They had almost seemed to be playing soldier at first—camping out, playing jokes, singing songs, raising hell. But now war's reality had caught up with them. The nostalgic longing for home, and the memories of the true childhood innocence of Christmases past, came flooding in at Christmastime 1862. A poem entitled "A Soldier's Christmas Eve" by an anonymous Northern soldier, published in the *Poughkeepsie Telegraph* on December 27, 1862, captured the longing for the bygone childhood innocence that Christmas now evoked in these men, who were no longer boys:

In a southern forest gloomy and old,
        So lately the scene of a terrible fight,
A soldier, alone in the dark and cold,
        Is keeping the watch tonight.
As he paces his round he sees the light
        Of his comrades' campfire, gleaming far,
        Through the dusky wood, and one bright star
Looks down with a twinkle of light and love
From the frosty sky that bends above.
        Large, clear and bright in the far-off skies
It twinkles and glimmers there alone
Like the blessed Bethlehem star that shone
        On the shepherd's wondering eyes.

As he watches it slowly, sweetly rise
His heart is touched by its gentle ray.
        And away, away,
His thoughts on the wings of fancy stray,
He forgets the night with its frosty air,
And cheerless blast, that every where

Moans loud through the branches black and bare,
He is thinking now of the little band
    In his boyhood home, whose faces bright
Are beaming with happiness as they stand
    Round the Christmas tree tonight,
And he seems to join with the happy throng
    In each innocent game and mirthful song.

Ah! vision as bright as fairy land!
    Like a broken dream, it will not stay,
He raises his weather-beaten hand
    And dashes a tear away.

And from a Southern soldier, William Gordon Mc-
Cabe, encamped with the Army of Northern Virginia,
came a poem that expressed almost exactly the same
sentiment. Entitled "Christmas Night of '62," it too
spoke of Christmases past, Christmases from a sim-
pler, more carefree time of life:

The wintry blast goes wailing by,
The snow is falling overhead;
I hear the lonely sentry's tread,
And distant watch-fires light the sky.

Dim forms go flitting through the gloom;
The soldiers cluster round the blaze
To talk of other Christmas days,
And softly speak of home and home.

. . .

My thoughts go wandering to and fro,
Vibrating between the Now and Then;
I see the low-browed home again,
The old hall wreathed with mistletoe.

And sweetly from the far-off years
Comes borne the laughter faint and low,
The voices of the Long Ago!
My eyes are wet with tender tears.

I feel again the mother-kiss,
I see again the glad surprise
That lightened up the tranquil eyes
And brimmed them o'er with tears of bliss,

As, rushing from the old hall-door,
She fondly clasped her wayward boy—
Her face all radiant with the joy
She felt to see him home once more.

In empty homes that Christmas, the optimism, or
at least stoic patriotism, of the year before was giving
way to more open thoughts of absence and loss too.
A lady in Richmond wrote:

The Christmas dinner passed off gloomily. The va-
cant chairs were multiplied in Southern homes, and
even the children who had so seriously questioned
the cause of the absence of the young soldier brother
from the festive board, had heard too much, had seen
too much, and knew too well why sad-colored garments were worn by the mother, and the fold of rusty
crape placed around the worn hat of the father, and
why the joyous mirth of the sister was restrained, and
her beautiful figure draped in mourning. Congratula-
tions were forced, and tears had taken the place of
smiles on countenances where cheerfulness was wont
to reign.

Tens of thousands were already dead. And in that
sheer onslaught of the dead, some of the enmity that
had been reserved for the enemy was numbed, for
the war was beginning to make everyone feel a victim. The war that had been a great cause was now

coming to seem like a faceless, malevolent force of nature—a kind of pestilence against which people of either side were powerless to stop. Some even dared to suggest that if anyone were to blame for the mounting toll of the dead, it was not damned Yankees or damned Rebels: it was the leaders of both sides who refused to make peace, who kept the war going by their incompetence, or by their insensibility to its terrible toll. One Confederate soldier, Tally Simpson of the 3rd South Carolina, wrote his sister from camp near Fredericksburg on Christmas Day 1862, very much in this vein:

My dear Sister,

This is Christmas Day. The sun shines feebly through a thin cloud, the air is mild and pleasant, a gentle breeze is making music through the leaves of the lofty pines that stand near our bivouac. All is quiet and still, and that very stillness recalls some sad and painful thoughts.

This day, one year ago, how many thousand families, gay and joyous, celebrating Merry Christmas, drinking health to absent members of their family, and sending upon the wings of love and affection long, deep, and sincere wishes for their safe return to the loving ones at home, but today are clad in the deepest mourning in memory to some lost and loved member of their circle. If all the dead (those killed since the war began) could be heaped in one pile and all the wounded be gathered together in one group, the pale faces of the dead and the groans of the wounded would send such a thrill of horror through the hearts of the originators of this war that their very souls would rack with such pain that they would prefer being dead and in torment than to stand before God with such terrible crimes blackening their characters. Add to this the cries and wailings of the mourners—mothers and fathers weeping for their sons, sisters for their brothers, wives for their husbands, and daughters for their fathers—how deep would be the convictions of their consciences.

Yet they do not seem to think of the affliction and distress they are scattering broadcast over the land. When will this war end?

⋰⋱

There were even some odd little acts of Christmas kindness between Yankees and Rebels that seemed to acknowledge a shared fate against the common enemy: the war itself, and the hardships it had brought.

In Winchester, Virginia, now occupied by Union troops, there lived the wife of a Confederate general. Her husband was in Richmond fighting for the South. The Confederate lady had started a dance class for the local boys and girls, and when Christmas came the pupils wanted to give their teacher a Christmas present. Together they managed to scrape up three dollars in Yankee greenbacks, which they hoped to use to buy some sugar, coffee, and tea. But the Union troops had forbade their sutlers to sell supplies to the locals for fear it would be used to aid the Confederate troops in the area. So five of the girls decided to go straight to the Union colonel and ask permission to buy their teacher's Christmas gift.

"You can hardly imagine a more scared set of little girls," recalled one of the girls who set down the story years later, but they bravely marched up to the sentinel in front of the officers' tent and asked to see the colonel—on "important business." Ushered in to the commander's presence, they explained their errand and were immediately set at ease when the colonel gently agreed to take care of the matter for them.

"That afternoon up came the colonel's orderly with twenty pounds of sugar and a large packet of coffee and tea (I suppose five times as much as our money would have bought) and a nice letter with three one-dollar greenbacks, saying that he was glad to contribute to the brave little girls who wished to give a Christmas present to the wife of a Confederate general who had given her time for our amusement."

It was a small incident, but one that that small Virginia girl never forgot, and never tired of telling for years after the war.

❧

As the sun set on Christmas Day 1862, it was hope for peace more than for victory that filled the hearts of war-weary soldiers and civilians, Northern and Southern alike. In New York City, lawyer George Templeton Strong wrote in his diary, "Christmas is a great institution, especially in time of trouble and disaster and impending ruin. *Gloria in Excelsis Deo et in Terra Pax* are words of permanent meaning independent of chance and change, and that meaning is most distinctively felt when war and revolution are shaking the foundations of society and threatening

respectable citizens like myself with speedy insolvency."

From the soldiers in a war that now seemed without end—men who daily faced a threat far more grave than "speedy insolvency"—the prayers on Christmas Day for peace resounded more tellingly. "Will another Christmas roll around and find us all wintering in camp?" Tally Simpson asked at the end of his Christmas letter to his sister. "Oh! That peace may soon be restored to our young but dearly beloved country and that we may all meet again in happiness."

Words expressing undiluted faith in the war's purpose were hard to find that bleak day. But there were some. One expression of faith came from the former slaves of the South Carolina sea islands who had been freed by the occupying Union forces. A Massachusetts officer, Colonel Thomas Wentworth Higginson, organized the freed slaves into one of the first black regiments, the 1st South Carolina Volunteers. On Christmas Day 1862, Higginson recorded in his diary the simple, hopeful hymn his men had sung that day:

We'll fight for liberty
Till de Lord shall call us home
We'll soon be free
Till de Lord shall call us home.

The poet Walt Whitman offered another expression of faith as he struggled to find meaning in so much death. It was a faith that tied the war to the most basic meaning of Christmas. But it was shocking nonetheless. Abandoning all high-minded pretense of martial glory and romance, shunning even the sentimental Christmas associations of home and boyhood nostalgia, Whitman looked death in the face in a way that would have seemed indelicate, even callous, a year earlier. But in confronting himself with the martyrdom of innocence that the war now daily brought, Whitman was led to think of Christ himself:

A sight in camp in the daybreak gray and dim,
As from my tent I emerge so early sleepless,
As slow I walk in the cool fresh air the path near by
   the hospital tent,

Three forms I see on stretchers lying, brought out there
    untended lying,
Over each the blanket spread, ample brownish woolen
    blanket,
Gray and heavy blanket, folding, covering all.

Curious I halt and silent stand,
Then with light fingers I from the face of the nearest the
    first just lift the blanket;
Who are you elderly man so gaunt and grim, with
    well-gray'd hair, and flesh all sunken about the eyes?
Who are you my dear comrade?

Then to the second I step—and who are you my child
    and darling?
Who are you sweet boy with cheeks yet blooming?

Then to the third—a face nor child nor old, very calm,
    as of beautiful yellow-white ivory;
Young man I think I know you—I think this face is the
    face of Christ himself,
Dead and divine and brother of all, and here again he
    lies.

2

AN AUTUMN OF
DISCONTENT

Disillusionment with war, with *the* war, had been growing steadily through the fall of 1862. There were many causes. But most of all was a creeping conviction that the war had become simply unwinnable.

The first Northern units to march off to war in April 1861 had been militiamen enlisted for ninety-day service. "On to Richmond!" Northern newspapers had trumpeted and the streets of every Northern city and town had filled with cheering throngs. "I never knew what a popular excitement could be," wrote a Harvard professor. "The whole population, men, women, and children, seem to be in the streets with Union favors and flags." Even Northern newspapers that had opposed Lincoln's election now closed ranks in patriotic fervor, calling for swift retribution against the rebels. "All squeamish sentimentality should be discarded," editorialized a Columbus, Ohio, newspaper, "and bloody vengeance wreaked upon the heads of the contemptible traitors who have provoked it by their dastardly impertinence and rebellious acts."

In thousands of letters and diaries, Union soldiers in those first days expressed an idealistic conviction in their cause and a certainty in its swift triumph. They were fighting "to maintain the best government on earth," wrote many. They owed it to their forebears who had paid for American freedom in the Revolution; they owed it to their descendants to pass on that freedom; they owed it to God to be true to this sacred trust.

Just before the First Battle of Bull Run, Sullivan Ballou of the 2nd Rhode Island Volunteers wrote to his wife a letter that would become famous after Ballou was killed in the battle. It was exceptional for its eloquent and poignant tone, but it spoke what countless others sincerely felt in those idealistic early days:

My very dear Sarah, The indications are very strong that we shall move in a few days—perhaps

tomorrow. Lest I should not be able to write you again, I feel impelled to write lines that may fall under your eye when I shall be no more ... If it is necessary that I should fall on the battlefield for my country, I am ready. I have no misgivings about, or lack of confidence in, the cause in which I am engaged, and my courage does not halt or falter. I know how strongly American Civilization now leans upon the triumph of the Government, and how great a debt we owe to those who went before us through the blood and suffering of the Revolution. And I am willing—perfectly willing—to lay down all my joys in this life, to help maintain this Government, and to pay that debt.

The enthusiasm, the idealism, and the expectation of swift and glorious victory, were no less strong in the South. "I am absent in a glorious cause, and glory in being in that cause," a Southern soldier assured his family in a letter he sent home soon after arriving in camp. "We have a country, at last, to live for, to pray for, to fight for, and if necessary to die for," proclaimed a Mississippian. The Southerners, too, saw themselves as heirs of the Revolutionary generation. As a New

Orleans poet wrote a month after the firing on Fort Sumter:

> Yes, call them rebels! 'tis the name
>   Their patriot fathers bore,
> And by such deeds they'll hallow it,
>   As they have done before.

Across the Southern states, recruiting meetings were mobbed. Many Southern boys were sure that they didn't have a moment to lose: if they didn't join up instantly, the war would be over and they would miss out on the "fun." No Southerners had doubts about the outcome. "Just throw three or four shells among those blue-bellied Yankees," said one North Carolinian, "and they'll scatter like sheep."

❧

The First Battle of Bull Run had convinced the North that this would be no ninety-day war. The recruits that replaced them were now required to enlist for three years. And then came the slow, grinding stalemate of 1862. Like a pair of charging bull moose, Northern and Southern armies crashed against one

another again and again, unable to gain permanent ground, unable to stop. Americans were killing each other at a staggering pace, yet the war was going nowhere. Second Bull Run, Seven Days, Shiloh, Antietam: each added to the grim toll, yet the stalemate only grew deeper.

"The romance of the thing is entirely worn off, not only with myself but with the whole army," wrote a soldier in Confederate general Stonewall Jackson's brigade. Another Confederate wrote, "I am sick and tired of this war, and I can see no prospects of having peace for a long time to come, I don't think it will ever be stopped by fighting, the Yankees can't whip us and we can never whip them, and I see no prospect of peace unless the Yankees themselves rebel and throw down their arms, and refuse to fight any longer."

In the summer of 1862, nearly one hundred thousand Union troops had advanced on Richmond up the Virginia Peninsula, only to grind to a halt within a few miles of the enemy capital. Later in the summer, General Robert E. Lee, commanding the newly formed Army of Northern Virginia, had tried to turn the tide by boldly taking the fight to the enemy's soil. But his invasion of Maryland had ended at Antietam, with the single bloodiest day of the war. It was a Confederate defeat, but it had cost the Union armies so dear that, stunned and reeling, they allowed Lee to escape what otherwise might have been certain destruction—what might even have brought the war to a close.

In the West, Confederate generals Braxton Bragg and Edward Kirby Smith had tried to reclaim Kentucky in a double-pronged thrust into that border state; those efforts too had ended in a strategic defeat for the Confederate forces, but one that had left the Union side almost as badly demoralized. The Southern press mercilessly denounced Bragg for retreating back to Tennessee. But the Northern press just as mercilessly condemned its generals for letting Bragg get away. In the demoralized spirit of the fall of 1862, battles no longer seemed to have victors at all.

❧

The stalemate and the demoralization were both, at least in part, a consequence of the modern weapons that reaped a grisly harvest of death with industrial efficiency.

The rifled musket, with its long range and high accuracy, now greatly favored the defense. Those who

persisted in valorous charges in close order were mowed down in numbers that defied imagination. In the old days of the smoothbore musket, troops *had* to advance in close order to concentrate the fire of those short-range and inaccurate weapons. The old muskets were effective only out to about eighty yards, so a brave charge with bayonets could often carry a line before the defenders could even reload and fire a second volley.

But the spinning bullets that blazed from the rifled barrels of the guns that all troops now carried had an effective range of three hundred, even four hundred yards. And so a charge had become something akin to a suicide mission. Some commanders realized this, but many were slow to grasp how much the old rules had changed. Even those who did realize it often saw no alternative. The long range of the rifle now made it impossible to support an infantry advance with artillery, as Napoleon had done with such éclat: the defenders could pick off the gunners and their horses before they even got in range. And so there seemed to be no other option but to send in waves of infantry in whatever numbers it took so that enough were left standing when the slaughter was through. "It was thought to be

a great thing to charge a battery of artillery or an earthwork lined with infantry," recalled Confederate general D. H. Hill some years later. "We were very lavish of blood in those days." Of one battle, where fifty-five hundred Confederates were killed and wounded as they charged into a Union artillery position atop a commanding slope, Hill grimly observed, "This was not war; it was murder."

At Fredericksburg in December 1862, the roles were reversed. Thirteen thousand Union troops were mowed down as wave after futile wave attempted to take a well-protected Confederate position on high ground. Afterward, a weary Union survivor lamented, "We have been worked hard and are nearly used up." One newspaper correspondent wrote, "It can hardly be in human nature for men to show more valor, or generals to manifest less judgment." *Harper's Weekly* declared that the country had borne "imbecility, treachery, failure, privation, loss of friends, but they cannot be expected to suffer that such massacres as this at Fredericksburg shall be repeated." Lincoln was thrown into the depths of despair by the news from Fredericksburg. "If there is a worse place than Hell," he said, "I am in it." A few days later, depressed still

more by rumors that had swirled through Washington of an impending revolt by dissatisfied members of his own party, the President said to a friend, "We are now on the brink of destruction. It appears to me that the Almighty is against us."

≈∽≈

By autumn's end, a deep bitterness had suffused the Union army. Men now were openly blaming their generals for the setbacks they had suffered, for the bravery that had been so callously expended. "Our poppycorn generals kill men as Herod killed the innocents," a Massachusetts private declared. A New York corporal wrote in a letter home, "Mother, do not wonder that my loyalty is growing weak. I am sick and tired of disaster and the fools that bring disaster upon us."

Soldiers began to grasp at rumors of a miraculous deliverance that would save them from any further fighting—always a sign of a thoroughly demoralized army. "We had a rumor here on Thursday that some of the rebel states had petitioned to be taken back into the Union and the authorities in Nashville fired a thirteen-gun salute in honor of it," wrote Illinois

soldier George G. Sinclair to his wife. "And also that General Lee had been sent from Richmond and power from the Confederacy to treat for an armistice for thirty days." But then Sinclair added, "I rather guess it's all moonshine with no foundation at all. In fact it is too good to be true."

In this climate, the resentments that the men in the ranks had always felt toward martial discipline swelled. As volunteers, and as proudly free Americans, most recruits had taken a rather casual attitude toward military courtesies and drill. The state militia units already in place when the war began were often little more than glorified drum and bugle corps or fraternal orders that spent as much time drinking as drilling. Few had experienced any real military duty. They often wore flamboyant uniforms and took exotic names for their regiments. All insisted on the old American tradition of electing their officers—who inevitably were chosen more for being good fellows than good disciplinarians.

After the first brush with real war there had been some fast readjustments. But still there remained for many soldiers, especially in the rougher units in the

West, an abiding resentment of having to follow orders.

Now those simmering resentments returned to the boil. In their Christmas letter to their father, the Searles brothers of the 21st Ohio had complained bitterly about the officers who were acting like so many "tyrants," they said. "For the whole of us as an army are used worse than the niggar ever was. And why is it? It is because all the tyrants of our nation have the command of the boys. Had we men of age and men that had been a private soldier himself for officers, one that had carried a knapsack and done duty as a soldier, then we might look for humane feelings shown towards us, but none now. But our 3 years is about 1/2 out now and then Mr. Officer will not wear so many feathers as they now do."

"Drill & saluting officers & guard duty is all played out," asserted one Massachusetts private. "All played out" became the sardonic catchphrase among Northern troops that fall. A regimental chaplain wrote, "The frenzy of our soldiers rushing to glory or death has, as our boys amusingly affirm, *been played out.*" The phrase also featured prominently in a doggerel song that soon swept the ranks, a play on the drinking song "Johnny, Fill Up the Bowl":

Abraham Lincoln, what yer 'bout?
Hurrah! Hurrah!
Stop this war. It's all played out.
Hurrah! Hurrah!

Abraham Lincoln, what yer 'bout?
Stop this war. It's all played out.
We'll all drink stone blind:
Johnny, fill up the bowl!

The other popular song that season was a melancholy air. It was as far from one of the many martial rallying songs that had been so popular the year before as a lullaby was from a bugled cavalry charge:

Many are the hearts that are weary tonight
Wishing for the war to cease
Many are the hearts looking for the right
To see the dawn of peace

Tenting tonight, tenting tonight
Tenting on the old campground

The defeatism and malaise that suffused the ranks alarmed the Union command. "The slumber of the army . . . is eating into the vitals of the nation," the quartermaster general of the Union army confessed privately in the late fall of 1862. "As day after day has gone, my heart has sunk and I see greater peril to our nationality in the present condition of affairs than I have seen at any time during the struggle."

❧❧❧

Ironically, the South was gripped by an almost identical sense of failure and despair. For one thing, the sting of war was now being felt firsthand by the very throngs who had cheeringly sent sons and husbands and brothers off to war the year before. When the summer Peninsula campaign brought war right to the outskirts of Richmond, the city was soon filled with thousands of wounded. "We lived in one immense hospital, and breathed the vapors of the charnel house," wrote a Richmond woman. Churches, hotels,

shops, and even private residences were used as hospitals. It was one thing for civilians to read their soldiers' letters describing the horror of war, quite another to see it for themselves on their very doorsteps, in their very homes.

In countless ways, life now grew increasingly difficult. The Confederacy was perpetually broke trying to finance the war. The states of the Confederacy had seceded from the Union on the principle of their individual sovereignty, and they now bridled at any attempts by their new federal authority to assert central power, especially over taxation. To help pay for the war, the Confederate congress imposed a direct tax on real estate, slaves, and other property, but left it to the states to collect it. Only a paltry $17.5 million came in. (Only South Carolina actually collected the tax; most of the other states just borrowed the money—or even printed up their own paper notes to cover their share.) The Confederate government also tried to raise money by selling bonds, but many of the bonds were simply bought with still other paper treasury notes issued by the government. In the end, three-quarters of the cost of the war was paid for by printing money, a mountain of $1.5 billion of worthless paper.

Inevitably, prices soared. And so the real burden of the war fell on the backs of the poor. By late 1862, the value of Confederate currency had dropped to less than fifteen cents on the dollar compared to where it had started. Prices of many staples shot beyond the reach of all but the wealthiest. Salt, a necessity for curing meat, went from two dollars a bag to sixty dollars. In New Orleans, flour was going for fifty-five dollars a barrel, shoes fifteen dollars a pair.

"There is now in this country much suffering amongst the poorer classes of Volunteers' families for want of *corn and salt*," wrote a Mississippian. "In the name of God, I ask is this to be tolerated? Is this war to be carried on and the Government upheld at the expense of the starvation of women and children?"

Several Southern states tried to stem the rising tide of inflation by passing laws setting maximum prices for food, but these only worsened the shortages as farmers refused to sell or black markets sprung up. In Richmond, the Confederate war department clerk John B. Jones, whose diary would became a famous account of life in the Confederate capital through these difficult days, noted that "none but the opulent can obtain a sufficiency of food and raiment." A few

months later he recorded that for want of food he had lost twenty pounds and his wife and children were "emaciated." He half jokingly suggested that maybe they would have to kill and eat the rats in his kitchen that had become so tame through hunger themselves that they would eat crumbs out of his daughter's hand, like kittens.

Even more consternation and class bitterness was caused by the controversial decision to impose a draft in the spring of 1862. The draft law was resented throughout the South, and even opposed by force in some places. The law exempted newspaper editors, pharmacists, ministers, teachers, and several other professions—which created a boom in "schools" teaching these careers, and in "apothecary shops" that sold little more than a few combs and brushes. The governors of North Carolina and Georgia, who violently objected to the draft's usurpation of states' rights, insisted that state militia officers were included in the draft law's exemption of state officials, and began naming hundreds of new officers. One Confederate general sarcastically described the result. The typical regiment from one of these states, he said, consisted

of "3 field officers, 4 staff officers, 10 captains, 30 lieutenants, and 1 private with a misery in his bowels."

But the most resented provision of the Confederate draft law was an exemption added in September 1862 that allowed one white man to remain on a plantation for every twenty slaves. The law effectively let the planter class and their overseers escape military service altogether. Though presented as a necessity to maintain social order and keep the land producing vitally needed crops, the "twenty negro law" fueled the flames of class resentment throughout the Confederacy. The law had had an instantaneous and "calamitous" effect on the poor, one southern senator warned President Jefferson Davis in December. Many became disillusioned not only with the conduct of the war, but with the Southern cause, period. "A rich man's war but a poor man's fight," became a popular cry.

"All they want is to git you to go fight for their infernal negroes," claimed one poor farmer, "and after you do their fightin' you may kiss their hine parts for all they care." Even many impassioned supporters of the Confederacy now denounced the "despotism" of the central government. Some even began to darkly mutter that it was just such a usurpation of rights that had led them to break with the Union. Now Jefferson Davis was acting as bad as the tyrant Lincoln—or worse.

><><

It was all too much for many a Southern soldier. The war was going nowhere; his family at home was starving; what good was it to fight a futile war for a cause that had seemed to desert the very men who had so loyally rallied to its side? In Bragg's Army of Tennessee, thousands of men deserted. By late fall an officer reported that "desertions are multiplying so fast in this army that almost one-third of it is gone."

Like his Northern counterpart, the common Confederate soldier was also growing disgusted with his leadership. Bragg's chaotic retreat from Kentucky had especially blackened his name with his officers and men. It had been a confusing fight in Kentucky, full of hopes of a much-needed Southern victory, but also full of miscalculation—and, said some, of simple cowardice on the part of Bragg.

The Confederate general was a strange study. A

West Point graduate, a hero of the Mexican War, where he had served as an able artillery officer under Zachary Taylor, Bragg was a tireless worker, a master of detail. He was also a stern disciplinarian—and a congenital hypochondriac, beset his whole life by a rash of chronic ills from headaches to dyspepsia. With his heavy eyebrows and haggard appearance, Bragg looked to one Georgia girl "like an old porcupine." She also thought him probably the "ugliest" man in the Confederate army.

He was certainly quarrelsome. He often seemed as irritable with himself as with those about him. Many of Bragg's critics had also noted a propensity for fatal hesitation at the moment of truth. Cutting off the Union army's line of retreat at a crucial juncture of the Kentucky campaign, he had suddenly abandoned his commanding position and let his enemy safely return to its base in Louisville. When a second opportunity for battle presented itself, and Kirby Smith begged him to join in a concerted attack, Bragg again hesitated—then finally withdrew.

Hundreds of sick and wounded men were abandoned by the retreating army. The retreat itself turned into a mess, "one of fearful suffering," related one soldier. "We were ordered to draw ten days' rations and march to Knoxville by way of Cumberland Gap. We failed to draw the rations as we did not overtake any provision-wagons and those we guarded were loaded with ordnance. For ten days we had nothing to eat save what we could find on the march through a mountainous and sparsely settled country"—land that had already been picked clean by both armies passing over the same ground earlier in the campaign. As the soldiers arrived in East Tennessee, conditions continued to deteriorate. A drought had ruined the crops, and an early winter storm in October covered the ground with six inches of snow. Hundreds of men, lacking winter clothing, blankets, or even shoes, died of exposure. The freezing air and a lack of adequate food set off epidemics of pneumonia, typhoid, and scurvy.

The retreat had also thrown Bragg's subordinate generals into a state of near rebellion. They wrote to Jefferson Davis seeking to have Bragg relieved of his command. "You are astonished at our exodus from Kentucky no doubt," Kirby Smith wrote his wife when it was all over. "No one could have

anticipated it—Bragg's movements since taking command in Kentucky have been most singular and unfortunate."

But Davis stubbornly defended his choice of Bragg and let it be known he would stay in command. The Confederate president told Kirby Smith that while other generals might "excite more enthusiasm," Bragg had organizational abilities that commended him to the job.

The more enthusiastic officers in the Army of Tennessee, who itched for a few actual victories, gnashed their teeth. A popular story went around the ranks about certain top civilian officials in Richmond: "If their souls had been tied up with red tape, indorsed in accordance with the latest orders, stuffed into pigeon holes, they would have preferred it to a guarantee of salvation." It was also said of "a certain Confederate general of high rank" that he would "rather have his subordinates submit a neat and formal report of a defeat than a slovenly account of victory."

And so the Confederate army that had straggled back into East Tennessee was torn by dissension among its officers and sapped by desertions and anger in the ranks.

⁂

What the men who clung to their duty on both sides of the endless war now so desperately needed was some reason to keep fighting—something worth fighting for.

If they could no longer look to their leaders or their cause to sustain them, then they would just have to look to themselves.

3

EVE OF BATTLE

urfreesboro was a neat, pretty, well-to-do town of some four thousand staunchly Southern citizens, located thirty miles southeast of Nashville in the heart of Middle Tennessee. From the elegant three-story-tall, white-painted cupola perched atop the large three-story brick courthouse in the town's center, a fine view could be had of the rich agricultural lands to which the town owed much of its prosperity.

The courthouse had been finished just a few years before the war, a testimony to the town's pride in its prosperity and success. It was the highest building by far, visible from miles away. It stood in the center of a square that divided the town's main street. To the east, elegant brick houses with flower-filled gardens and magnolia trees stood along streets lined with stately elms and oaks. Just a few blocks from the courthouse, a half-mile-long carriage lane led north to the plantation owned by descendants of the town's founder and namesake. Oaklands was one of the most beautiful residences in Middle Tennessee, an Italianate mansion that stood at the center of a 215-acre tract, part of a larger plantation of fifteen hundred acres with nearly a hundred slaves producing wheat, corn, and oats.

Winding to the north of Murfreesboro in gentle sweeping meanders, Stones River—named after an early explorer—flowed into the Cumberland River at Nashville. The river, no less than the soil, had been the making of Murfreesboro and surrounding Rutherford County. Boats had carried away the cotton, tobacco, and cedar logs produced by the first settlers. From places as distant as New Orleans and Pittsburgh, they had carried back the necessities and luxuries that the increasingly prosperous planters demanded—bacon, salt, nails, gunpowder; whiskey, brandy, linens, silk.

Now a network of macadamized turnpike roads radiated from Murfreesboro around the compass:

northwest to Nashville, northeast to Lebanon, southwest to Salem, west to Triune. Since 1851 they had been joined by the Nashville and Chattanooga Railroad, the main line linking Tennessee to the South Atlantic states. Running almost, but not quite, parallel to the arrow-straight line of the Nashville Pike, the equally straight railroad crossed the Pike at an acute angle about two miles north of town.

It was primarily to guard the railroad that a force of two thousand Union soldiers had occupied this sedate crossroads town in March of 1862. In spite of a hostile populace that had adamantly refused to cooperate with the occupiers, the Union troops had grown complacent. The nearest Rebel force of any size was said to be in Chattanooga, 150 miles away.

And so early on a sleepy summer morning, Sunday, July 13, 1862, Union soldiers were startled awake by a thundering of hoofs that heralded the entry of fourteen hundred troopers led by the soon-to-be-legendary Confederate cavalry commander Nathan Bedford Forrest. Soon a column was galloping up the lane to Oaklands, where the 9th Michigan Infantry was encamped under the shade of the large oaks on the front lawn that gave the plantation its name. In the skirmish that ensued, the regiment's colonel was wounded and carried into the house.

There promptly followed a written demand from Forrest himself. "Colonel: I must demand the unconditional surrender of your force as prisoners of war or I will have every man put to the sword. You are aware of the overpowering force I have at my command, and this demand is made to prevent the effusion of blood. I am, Colonel, very respectfully, your obedient servant, N. B. Forrest, Brigadier General of Cavalry, C.S. Army." The Yankees surrendered, and that evening Forrest's men were on their way again, leaving as fast as they had come.

Hearing the news of Forrest's raid on Murfreesboro, and fearing a threat to their hold on the state's capital itself, the Union army at Nashville quickly pulled back the forces they had too confidently spread all across Middle and West Tennessee. For the rest of the summer and fall the Union army would remain encamped in and around Nashville, behind strong fortifications.

And so it was to Murfreesboro that Bragg now, in late fall, decided to concentrate his entire Army of Tennessee. He hoped to entice the Union army into a battle in which Bragg would hold the defensive advantage. Murfreesboro was unquestionably a strategic point of importance. And the still-productive farms of the Stones River Valley had harvested an abundant crop this year that could feed his hungry troops.

But from a tactical point of view, Bragg could hardly have chosen worse. Rivers and hills just a few miles to the south formed a natural defensive line that would have been nearly impregnable had Bragg chosen to take up his position there. Murfreesboro itself, however, offered no natural advantages of terrain and a good many disadvantages. For one thing, the town could easily be outflanked by several good roads that paralleled the Nashville-to-Murfreesboro turnpike. But worst of all, defending Murfreesboro required spreading a force out across a fifty-mile front to patrol all of the compass-point roads leading to the town. Stones River bisected the potential front Bragg would have to defend north of the town, and that meant placing troops east and west of a river whose suddenly rising waters might cut off one half of his force from the other. The terrain north of Murfreesboro, a confusing patchwork of small cotton fields and dense cedar "brakes" filled with large, jagged limestone outcroppings, was about as rough and wild and confusing a landscape to fight a battle on as one could find anywhere.

⨀

Soldiers in the West, Johnnie Reb and Billy Yank alike, constantly chafed under the feeling that their efforts were going unappreciated by the politicians back East who were running the war, and whose attention was focused so intently on events along the Potomac. It didn't help that so many of the West Point graduates who commanded the Western armies were contemptuous of volunteer soldiers in general, and the ragtag Westerners in particular. Bragg all but openly disdained the Tennessee and Kentucky Confederate regiments, making it clear he thought they were poor fighters whose loyalty could not even be trusted.

In the Union army, the independent-minded and self-reliant young farm boys and frontiersmen from the Northwest who filled the regiments from Michigan, Ohio, and Indiana had come to nurture a particular grudge against their commander in the Kentucky fighting. He was a Regular Army major general with

the slightly ludicrous name of Don Carlos Buell. Buell had made plain that, as far as he was concerned, what the volunteers needed was a good dose of Regular Army discipline. All that did was to increase the men's contempt for following orders that reduced them to "mere machines." "The volunteer soldier could be led by justice, kindness and sympathy up to any point of excellence," recalled one veteran after war, "but was made sullen and disobedient by what was thought to be injustice or tyranny."

But with events in the West now approaching a strategic crisis, Western politicians in both the North and the South began to press Washington and Richmond to reverse the months of neglect, to repair as quickly as they could the damage that had been done in this now-suddenly critical theater of the war. The fulcrum of the entire war indeed appeared to have shifted westward: Union forces under U. S. Grant were pushing down the Mississippi River, threatening to split the Confederacy in two. In Tennessee, a Union victory would open the way for a drive through Georgia, further bisecting the South.

In early December 1862, Governor J. J. Pettus of Mississippi wired a plea to President Davis begging him to make a personal visit to the West: "You have often visited the army of Virginia. At this critical juncture could you not visit the army of the West? Something must be done to inspire confidence." Senator James Phelan of Mississippi added his voice, even asking Davis to take command of the army in the field himself:

The present alarming crisis in this state, so far from arousing the people, seems to have sunk them in listless despondency. The spirit of enlistment is thrice dead. Enthusiasm has expired to a cold pile of damp ashes. Defeats, retreats, sufferings, dangers, magnified by spiritless helplessness and an unchangeable conviction that our army is in the hands of ignorant and feeble commanders, are rapidly producing a sense of settled despair. . . . I imagine but one event that could awaken from its waning spark the enthusiastic hopes and energy of Mississippians. Plant your own foot upon our soil, unfurl your banner at the head of the army, tell your own people that you have come to share with them the perils of this dark hour. . . . If ever your presence was needed as a last refuge from an "Iliad of woes," this is the hour. It is not a point to

be argued. [Only] you can save us or help us save ourselves from the dread evils now so imminently pending.

On December 10, Davis slipped out of Richmond incognito—to avoid setting off rumors that the Southern capital was about to fall—and boarded a train for a long, circuitous ride to Chattanooga, where he arrived late in the evening. The next day he continued on to Murfreesboro by rail. By now news of the President's arrival had spread throughout Tennessee. His journey became practically a royal procession. Crowds packed way stations along the route to wave and cheer the President's train. At Murfreesboro, Davis was driven to Oaklands plantation and installed in the finest guest room of the house, with a fine view over the front lawn where Forrest, back in July, had captured the Union colonel.

That night a large and enthusiastic crowd came to serenade the President. He replied with a stirring speech full of confidence in the inevitability of a Confederate victory and urging the people to rise up and expel the invader who now occupied their soil. Davis also took the occasion to personally confer a

promotion to brigadier general upon the dashing cavalry colonel whose recent feats were on the lips of all the citizens of Murfreesboro. Colonel John H. Morgan had just led a daring raid by four small cavalry and two infantry regiments which had captured 1,762 prisoners and seized thousands of dollars' worth of supplies from a Union position forty miles upstream of Nashville along the Cumberland River.

But visits by great men cut two ways. A top Confederate general who had inspected Bragg's dispositions around Murfreesboro a few days earlier had been appalled. Privately he confided to a friend that if the Union army's general in Nashville "had disposed our troops himself, their disposition could not have been more unfavorable to us." But Davis had come to inspire confidence, and confidence was what he was determined to find. He wired his secretary of war back in Richmond: "Found the troops there in good condition and fine spirits. Enemy is kept close in to Nashville, and indicates only defensive purposes."

Davis decided that things were in such good shape at Murfreesboro, in fact, that he would transfer one of Bragg's seven divisions to Mississippi, where it was more urgently needed. Bragg strenuously objected,

but Davis insisted that there was little likelihood the Union troops would advance out of Nashville. When Bragg and the other generals continued to protest, Davis ordered them point-blank to issue the order at once to transfer the troops.

On December 13 the Confederate president headed on to Mississippi, where he regaled more cheering crowds with invectives against the "vandal hordes," which, so long as there was a God in heaven, would be hurled back from the sacred soil of the South.

Davis was not indulging in entirely wishful thinking in insisting that the troops were in good condition and spirits. Their sojourn at Murfreesboro had been a marked improvement over the recent hardships the Army of Tennessee had endured. The weather in Middle Tennessee had been unusually mild throughout November and early December. Convinced they would remain at Murfreesboro unmolested until spring, the men began to build more permanent and comfortable winter quarters in the form of rough log cabins, complete with fireplaces and chimneys.

Morgan's feats of arms had also raised spirits, of

soldiers and citizens alike. And then the dashing cavalry officer's wedding to a young local lady the day after Davis's departure heralded the start of a week and a half of Christmas festivities among the social elite of the town and the army. The story of Morgan's courtship and marriage was a perfect Southern romance of chivalry and gallantry. The thirty-six-year-old Morgan was the classic Southern aristocrat, six feet tall, handsome, a devotee of the Southern code of honor. He had been expelled from college for dueling. He also had a reputation as a gambler and a libertine, as well as a daring cavalry officer.

Mattie Ready was twenty-one, the daughter of one of the most prominent Rutherford County families. Her father, Colonel Charles Ready, Jr., had been a United States congressman before the war, and Mattie had become a favorite in Washington society while living there with her family.

In early March 1862, "the famous Captain Morgan" had been invited to dinner at the Ready home in Murfreesboro. Mattie had been asked to sing for their guest to cheer him up; his wife had recently died. Mattie's sister Alice described the evening in her diary the next day: "Morgan is an extremely modest man,

but very pleasant and agreeable, though to see him one would scarcely imagine him to be the daring reckless man he is. An immense crowd collected at the front door to see him, two or three actually came in and stood before the parlor door."

That did not sound like an especially conducive atmosphere to conduct a courtship, but Morgan found a better opportunity two weeks later. Spotting a Union cavalry regiment conducting a reconnaissance outside the town late one night as he was returning from an expedition, Morgan sent a servant to carry a note to Miss Ready asking whether the town was clear of the enemy. She immediately replied: "They are eight miles from here. Come in haste." Morgan came, and the two talked until daybreak. When he left, they were engaged. As he departed, Morgan formed his soldiers on the square in front of the house and led them in a chorus of "Cheer, Boys, Cheer."

A few months later, with Murfreesboro under Union occupation, Mattie chanced to overhear some of the Northern officers making disparaging remarks about Morgan. She interrupted them and began so vehemently to defend Morgan that one of the officers demanded to know her name. "It's Mattie Ready now," she replied haughtily, "but by the grace of God, one day I hope to call myself the wife of John Morgan!"

Their wedding on December 14 was one of the great social events not only of Murfreesboro, but of the entire Confederacy. The ceremony took place in one of the large parlors of the Readys' grand house. The entire headquarters staff, including General Bragg himself, was in attendance. So was Major General John C. Breckinridge, former vice president of the United States, now the most influential division commander in the Confederate army. One of the other generals who was present recalled the event for a newspaper reporter some years later:

All the officers of high rank who could reach Murfreesboro had assembled for the wedding. The house was packed with people to its full capacity, and decorated with holly and winterberries. The lights from lamps and candles flashed on the uniforms and the trappings of the officers, and were reflected in the bright eyes of the pretty Tennessee girls who had gathered. The raven-haired, black-mustached Morgan, in his general's uniform, looking like a hero of chivalry; the bride, a girl of rare beauty, tall, dark-haired, and blue-eyed, with a creamy complexion and perfect features; and standing before them, to perform the ceremony, in his full military uniform, Bishop Polk, himself a general of the Confederate Army and Bishop of the Episcopal Church. Miss Ready's bridal dress was one of her best antebellum frocks, for it was not possible at that time to purchase material for a trousseau.

General Morgan's attendants were as dashing a set of young soldiers as any bride could wish at her wedding.

Two or three regimental bands had been provided for the occasion. They were stationed in the house and on the porch, and there was plenty of music. Outside in the streets thousands of soldiers were assembled, who by the lighted bonfires, celebrated the wedding in proper style, cheering Morgan and his bride.

Colonel Ready's cellar still had a sufficient stock of wine to provide for the many toasts proposed to the happy couple.

The nearly two thousand Yankee prisoners that Morgan had brought into Murfreesboro just a few days before came to be known as "General Morgan's wedding present to the bride."

A week after the wedding Morgan was off again on another daring cavalry raid, this time to burn the trestles of the Louisville and Nashville Railroad north of Bowling Green.

Morgan thus missed the other great event of the Murfreesboro Christmas season, a grand ball given by the 1st Louisiana and 6th Kentucky regiments at the town's courthouse. The officers and the ladies of the town had gone all out to make it as glittering— and socially exclusive—an affair as they could. Only generals and colonels and their ladies were permitted inside the courthouse; lesser officers were restricted to the general festivities in the town square outside.

A participant described the scene within:

The decorations of the hall were magnificent, and constructed with much taste and ingenuity. And if "bright lamps" did not shine over "fair women and

brave men," at least many candles did—behind each one a bayonet, which brightly reflected the light on the festive scene.

There were trees of evergreens with colored lanterns in them in the corners of the hall, and flowers contributed by the Murfreesboro ladies, on the window-sills. There were two "B's" entwined in evergreen, on one side of the hall, representing Bragg and Breckinridge, while just below it hung a magnificent regimental flag.

Above the windows, also fashioned from evergreen, were the names of recent Confederate victories. And throughout the hall were "a good many splendid trophies from the different battle fields"—Yankee flags, captured by Morgan and his cavalrymen on their raids, and donated for the occasion by the new Mrs. Morgan. One young captain, Spencer Talley, was raring to attend the dance. Luckily his colonel had no interest in going himself and happily lent his own colonel's uniform to the young officer to secure his admittance. Talley recorded that he had "a most delightful time. We had the best band of musicians in the army and our

table was loaded with the best things that Murfrees-boro could afford."

The Christmas Eve party was still going strong when a rider suddenly broke upon the scene with startling news. The Yankees in Nashville were preparing to move. All indications were that that the Union army, which Bragg and Davis had confidently predicted would remain in place all winter, was about to march on Murfreesboro. Officers and couriers at once excused themselves and dashed off in every direction, leaving the young ladies of the ball to fend for themselves.

❧

The Union army was moving because it had a new leader.

Don Carlos Buell had lost the confidence not only of his men but of President Lincoln. "Not a moment too soon," cabled the governors of Indiana and Illinois when word came at the end of October that Lincoln had relieved Buell of his command. Just as Mississippi's governor and senator had frantically pressed Davis to show his support for the war effort in the West with some dramatic gesture, so the North-

ern governors had warned Lincoln that "in the Northwest distrust and despair are seizing upon the hearts of the people," and some bold steps were required. Getting rid of Buell was the breath of hope they had been praying for.

"You don't know how pleased everybody is at the change," wrote a Wisconsin officer of the dismissal of Buell. "We are glad to be delivered of Buell," agreed the sergeant major of the 51st Indiana. "There was silent rejoicing everywhere," said a soldier of the 15th Ohio.

The new Union commander, though, was almost as eccentric a study as the Confederates' Bragg. General William S. Rosecrans had graduated fifth in his class at West Point. He was a thinker and a scholar. But he also had a reputation for a kind of almost manic excitability. In conferences with his staff he could quote authorities on the principles of war and draw analogies to great events in military history. But in the heat of battle he often became so excited, and talked so fast, that he became almost incomprehensible.

He certainly had his share of detractors. The secretary of war had counseled against choosing so eccentric a man as Rosecrans for such an important command, acidly telling Lincoln after he had made the

appointment, "Well, you have made your choice of idiots. Now you can await news of a terrible disaster."

Many of Rosecrans's idiosyncrasies had to do with his late-found religious enthusiasm. Rosecrans had converted to Catholicism while a cadet at West Point, against the strenuous objections of his Methodist parents. He had all the proverbial zeal of a convert. He thoroughly immersed himself in the teachings of his new faith. A Catholic priest who had become his personal and spiritual confidant even accompanied the general in the field, performing Mass in his tent. The general himself often kept his whole staff up long after midnight in theological discussions, such as one devoted to the difference between profanity and blasphemy. (A great practitioner of the former, he always insisted he drew a personal line at the latter.) Rosecrans once kept his staff up half the night for ten nights running on one theological disputation. He insisted an efficient officer needed little sleep. But his staff noticed that Rosecrans himself would sleep till noon on such occasions. The general was also said to be a great drinker.

But his energy was unquestionably infectious. He seemed to be everywhere, fixing problems, chatting

with privates, offering bits of homey advice. "Boys, when you drill, drill like thunder. It is not the number of bullets you shoot, but the accuracy of the aim that kills more men in battle." He instituted discipline, but the kind the common soldier could respect. Special privileges for officers were curtailed. Everyone, officers and enlisted men alike, had to show a written pass when outside camp. Incompetent officers were cashiered and marched off in front of their troops. Troops drilled morning, noon, and night. Spotting a private without a canteen, the general demanded to know why he had not obtained a replacement. When the private said he had already asked for one, Rosecrans told the man to pester his captain until he got it. "Bore him for it! Bore him in his quarters! Bore him at his mealtime! Bore him in bed! Bore him; bore him; bore him." The boring would go up the line until it reached General Rosecrans himself, he assured the private, and "I'll see then if you don't get what you want."

Morale slowly began to pick up. There were still plenty of complaints and miseries, but at least the men now began to feel they had a leader who cared about them, whom they could trust. In mid-December a sort

of wandering minstrel had appeared in the camps at Nashville. He claimed to have a pass from Abraham Lincoln himself permitting him to travel throughout the armies of the West to boost morale. He would stand on a cracker barrel and sing patriotic songs. It would later turn out that the man, who called himself William E. Lock, was actually a Southern spy, and he would eventually be shot trying to run a picket line. But for now, at least, his cover was a good one. He always had his finger on the pulse of the common soldier's mood. And that mood in December 1862 in the camps around Nashville was an unabashed enthusiasm for the fact that at last they seemed to have a real leader in charge of them. Lock's most popular number was a rousing tribute to General Rosecrans, and when he called on the men to join in the chorus, thousands of voices bellowed out:

Old Rosy is the man, Old Rosy is the man!
We'll show our deeds where'er he leads;
Old Rosy is the man!

If the Rebels thirty miles away in Murfreesboro were content to stay all winter in their log cabins

enjoying the company of the local society, the Union army had good reason to cut its stay in Nashville as short as possible. Nashville was becoming an increasingly difficult place to hold. The citizenry was actively hostile. Under the military occupation, business had ground to a halt, the streets were filthy, crime was rampant, and many a soldier and officer gave way to the temptations of the readily available supplies of liquor and the fifteen hundred prostitutes who had flocked to the city. Food and coal remained short throughout the fall as Rebel cavalry raids harassed Union supply lines. The army had its hands full keeping order in the city—and trying to keep its own men in line.

Rosecrans had been brought in in large measure because Lincoln had grown exasperated with generals, like Buell, who were reluctant to attack. It had been the same story with General George B. McClellan, the much revered general of the Army of the Potomac, who had kept preparing and preparing and never moving until Lincoln at last fired him. But now Rosecrans seemed to be afflicted with the same ailment. Orders from the war department in Washington kept arriving, urging him to get on with it. But Rosecrans

sedately replied that he would do so only when he was ready. More worryingly, he started to insist that his inaction was brilliant strategy. It would "lull" the rebels into a false sense of security, Rosecrans explained, so that when he finally did move he would catch the enemy by surprise and finish them off.

In Washington, the need for a Union battlefield victory was becoming urgent. Lincoln's cabinet was in near revolt. The British and French were inching toward diplomatic recognition of the South, a step Lincoln feared would seal the South's independence.

In early December, the U.S. army's general in chief, Henry W. Halleck, finally lost all patience with Rosecrans and telegraphed an ultimatum: "The President is very impatient at your long stay in Nashville. The favorable season for your campaign will very soon be over. You give Bragg time to supply himself by plundering the very country your army should have occupied. Twice have I been asked to designate someone else to command your army. If you remain one more week in Nashville I cannot prevent your removal. As I wrote when you took the command, the Government demands action, and if you cannot respond to that demand someone else will be tried."

Rosecrans shot back an ill-tempered reply of his own. "I need no other stimulus to make me do my duty than the knowledge of what it is," he huffily informed his superior. "To threats of removal or the like I must be permitted to say that I am insensible."

Halleck in turn sent a calmer reply attempting to smooth Rosecrans's ruffled feathers; he never intended to imply "threats of removal or the like." But he explained the "great anxiety" in Washington to reverse the gains the Confederacy had made in Middle Tennessee since the summer. Driving the rebels out of the state would go a long way toward nipping the European diplomatic moves in the bud, before the British parliament was due to assemble in mid-January.

Rosecrans got the message. He had now accumulated five weeks of supplies. December rains had raised the Cumberland River sufficiently to allow Union gunboats to move up and down the river and keep that supply line open even if rebel cavalry continued to wreak havoc with the rail lines. And then came word about the departure of one of Bragg's divisions at Jefferson Davis's orders. Morgan's and Forrest's cavalries were also reported to be hundreds of miles away on expeditions in Kentucky and West Tennessee.

On Christmas Day, Rosecrans met with his corps commanders to review the situation. The discussion went on for some time. Finally the general leapt up from the table, slammed down the mug of toddy he had been drinking, and in a voice rushing with excitement practically shouted, "We move tomorrow, gentlemen! Press them hard! Drive them out of their nests! Make them fight or run! *Fight them! Fight them!* Fight, I say!"

4

"HOME! SWEET HOME!"

Morale had improved in both armies since its low point in late summer and fall, but it still remained in a tenuous state. Though creature comforts had taken a turn for the better in Bragg's Army of Tennessee and confidence had been bolstered in Rosecrans's Union ranks, the gnawing doubts about what they were fighting for still ate at men on both sides. The romance of war was certainly gone for good. That victory was still even possible seemed doubtful. That it was worth fighting and dying, or for that matter just putting up with all the miseries and insults of life as a common soldier, to defend an abstract notion like union or liberty—that was certainly "all played out."

Now with the battle in Tennessee about to be

joined at last, much of the bitterness on both sides came sweeping back. On the Confederate side, no one was to blame for the plummeting morale that gripped the army on the very eve of battle but Bragg himself.

Bragg had always been a stern disciplinarian. He had once had a man shot, it was said, for killing a chicken. The real story was more complicated. To conceal their movement from the enemy, Bragg had ordered absolute silence on the march. The unfortunate soldier, who was apparently a bit drunk, had decided to take a few shots at a chicken that he had spotted by the roadside. The chicken got away. But by firing his gun he had given away the army's presence, an act that might have endangered the lives of more than just one chicken. Bragg ordered the man be made an example of, and he was indeed shot. But that was not the message the troops got. The story everyone believed was that Bragg had had some poor fellow shot for nothing more than killing a chicken.

Yet soldiers' rumors have a way of capturing the essential truth. And the essential truth about Bragg was that he was rigid, domineering, and all too contemptuous of his own troops. He now proceeded to

confirm his reputation as the most callous commander in the Confederate army.

There was no doubt that the Army of Tennessee had been plagued by desertions and unauthorized leave-taking. But Bragg's solution showed how little sense he had of the deep and incurable resentments he was creating. Ever since the ill-fated venture in Kentucky, Bragg had been feuding with Breckinridge. It was typical of Bragg that he looked for someone else to blame for his own failures, and he pinned most of the blame for the failed expedition on Breckinridge and his fellow Kentuckians—who, Bragg went so far to say, were a bunch of ingrates and cowards who hadn't even lifted a finger to liberate their own state from the yoke of Yankee oppression. Bragg seemed to be spoiling to make an example of some of the Kentucky soldiers, and just before Christmas he apparently found it, in the case of a young private from the 6th Kentucky accused of desertion.

If ever there were grounds for leniency, Asa Lewis's case had them. Lewis had served gallantly in the battle of Shiloh, but had declined to reenlist when his term had expired several months earlier. Nonetheless he had stayed on in Murfreesboro until December and had finally agreed to sign up for another term of enlistment when suddenly word reached him that his father had died and his now-widowed mother's home had been burned to the ground by the Yankees. Lewis asked permission for leave to go visit her; the request was denied. He left anyway and headed for Kentucky. Caught on the road, he was brought back to Murfreesboro and warned not to try it again. But Lewis did try it again, and was caught again. This time he was sentenced to be shot by a firing squad.

Bragg rebuffed repeated appeals by Breckinridge and his officers to commute the sentence. Moreover, Bragg ordered the entire Kentucky brigade to assemble the morning after Christmas Day to witness the execution. Kentucky blood, he contemptuously told Breckinridge, was too feverish for the health of his army, and he would stop the Kentuckians' insubordination and complaining if he had to shoot every last one of them. Breckinridge retorted that the execution of Lewis was tantamount to murder.

Johnny Green, one of the Kentucky soldiers forced to witness Lewis's execution, described the ordeal in a letter he wrote the day afterward. "The whole division was formed in three sides of a square. Poor

Lewis was brought from prison in a wagon riding on his coffin and a detail of twelve men was made to shoot him. All was ready. He asked General Breckinridge for permission to say only a few words to the detail." Lewis spoke calmly to the men in the firing squad. "Comrades, I know you are all grieved to do this work but don't be distressed; none of you will know who kills me for you know one of your guns has no ball in it. Each man may think his was the harmless gun. But I beg you to aim to kill when the command 'fire' is given: it will be merciful to me. Good bye."

A cold, pelting rain had begun to fall over the field outside of town where the men had assembled for the grim spectacle. A dead silence fell. Then the lieutenant in command of the firing squad gave the order. "Ready. Aim. Fire." Twelve guns cracked. "All was over and a gloom settled over the command," wrote Green. Breckinridge himself was "seized with a deathly sickness" as the shots rang out, recalled a witness, "dropped forward on the neck of his horse, and had to be caught by some of his staff."

The Kentuckians were not the only ones to harbor resentments at Bragg's hard dealings. A whole series of executions took place in the days around Christmas even as the officers were amusing themselves with gala balls. The members of the 24th Tennessee threatened to desert en masse if Bragg carried out the death sentence against one of their members who had been convicted of desertion. "The grave had been dug, the troops of the brigade and division were all in position on the conventional three sides of a hollow square," recalled one soldier. "The wagon had driven up with the man seated on his coffin; the firing squad had taken position ten paces in front of the doomed victim, who had been blindfolded and placed at the grave, when an officer dashed up, his horse in a foam of sweat, with a reprieve." Apparently a man who could prove the innocence of the charge had ridden all night and day, nearly killing his horse, and the court martial had reversed the sentence at literally the last minute.

But most of the condemned men were not so lucky. An Alabama soldier was shot a few days before Christmas. "It was horrible," related a fellow soldier. "Owing to some blunder, the squad fired three

volleys into him before he was killed. It made a deep impression." Another Alabama soldier, E. P. Norman of the 28th Alabama, was, like Asa Lewis, shot the day after Christmas. He left a wrenching letter to his wife and children that he wrote on Christmas Day:

My Dear and Affectionate Wife and Little Children.
I for the last time seat myself to write you a few lines to let you know that I have heard my sentence and it is death. I am to be shot tomorrow the 26th. Dear wife and children, I see that I must die and I never on earth can meet you any more, but thank God I have faith to believe that I will meet you in a better world. . . .

Dear wife, I want you to get along the best you can and not grieve for me for we all have got to die sooner or later. This world is a world of trials and tribulations, our pleasures are now done on this earth but I hope we will meet in heaven where parting will be no more. Dear wife, I want you to try to raise my children right, treat them as well as you can and teach them to put their trust in God who is able to save them. . . . The time is fast approaching. It looks hard after going through the fatigue that I have and exposure trying to defend the rights of my country and after all I must now be put to death for going home to make some necessary preparations for my little family while others that left at the same time are not even arrested.

The next day Norman scribbled a few more hasty lines just as he was about to be taken away to be shot. "I have given my pocket book to James M. Tidwell with $2.25 in it to send to you and two small pieces of tobacco, my pocket knife and my clothes, all but these I have on. Give my knife to little Stephen and dear son, it's the best thing your papa ever expects to give you and I want you to keep it in remembrance of me. I want you all to be good children and mind your mother and try to conduct yourselves here on earth so when you come to die you will be prepared to meet God in peace. . . . Dear wife the time has arrived when I must go to the place of execution. . . . So good bye for awhile, E. P. Norman."

❧❧

Rosecrans's troops meanwhile encountered their own discontents as they began to prepare to meet their enemy. As late as Christmas Day the weather had remained unseasonably warm and fair. "The weather is so mild that we can write with comfort in the tent without a fire," wrote Arza Bartholomew, Jr., of the 21st Michigan to his wife on December 25. "If it doesn't get any colder than it is now, it will not be very bad."

But as Rosecrans's forty-four thousand troops received their orders to march several hours before daybreak on December 26, the weather took a terrible and rapid turn for the worse. At first light, heavy dark clouds could be seen hanging low on the horizon and a thick mist blanketed the camps. The wind turned and began to blow chill blasts from the west. As the first troops got under way a heavy rain began to fall.

The three wings of the army were ordered to head south toward Murfreesboro on separate, roughly parallel routes that took them on roads that varied from good macadamized turnpikes to rough country lanes. But soon the roads, good and bad alike, became an indistinguishable mire. "It began to rain and continued the balance of the day," wrote one Indiana soldier. "The hitherto dusty pike was converted into a sloppy sea of mud." Another unit reported that the road they had been assigned to follow had deteriorated to "the consistency of cream or very thick paste." Henry V. Freeman wrote in his notebook simply, "Worst mud I ever walked in."

Burdened down with a load that might have better suited a pack mule, the soldiers had a miserable time of it. "Each man is calculated to carry half a tent besides his knapsack, with a blanket and a shirt or two and a pair of drawers, socks, and overcoat, canteen, haversack, and cartridge box with 20 rounds and gun besides," wrote soldier James S. McCarty. "So you can see it is a load to carry and march 15 or 20 miles a day."

The landscape between Nashville and Murfreesboro might have seemed pretty in fairer weather and better days, but to the troops slogging their way south it looked like "a perfect wilderness waste," one soldier wrote. All along the way were burned-out houses from earlier clashes and raids, ghostly ruins with nothing but a chimney left standing. The Union troops were constantly harassed by small bands of Confederate skirmishers who fell slowly back to Murfreesboro

ahead of the advancing Federals. In the distance was the steady, ominous rumble of cannon.

Repeatedly, the roads become clogged by bogged-down supply trains—"a tangled mass of mules and wagons," as one newspaper correspondent on the scene described it. Units lost their way as they sought out drier ground by cutting across fields and woods. Even Rosecrans and his staff got lost at one point and found themselves trotting aimlessly over "rugged narrow lanes and gloomy forests, upon unknown paths, which but an hour ago had rattled under the hoofs of Rebel horsemen," according to a war correspondent who traveled with the general. Rosecrans finally jumped a fence at the edge of a field and took off across a thick forest on the other side, with a few alarmed staff officers following in his wake. They managed to reach their intended destination for the night at one A.M.

Nights on the march offered little rest for the weary soldiers. "Toward night it just poured down in torrents," recalled James McCarty. Some tried to find a comfortable spot between the rows of corn in the fields, but that turned out to be a mistake. "To make things pleasant we were allowed no fire and it rained very heavy during the night," wrote George Sinclair. "In the morning I found myself laying right in a pool of water as each hollow between the corn ridges was full." The only food they had to sustain them was the three days' rations the men carried with them—a pound of hardtack and three-quarters of a pound of salt pork apiece.

"During the march to Murfreesboro, it was nothing but a continual rain day and night, so that we were wet through," recalled Amandus Silsby of the 24th Wisconsin. "The roads were full of mud and slush, so the four days before the fight my feet were wet soaking all the time. Monday night all that was left of my shoes gave way, so that I had to go it barefoot."

By the night of Tuesday, December 30, the advancing army at last found itself a few miles north of Murfreesboro. The courthouse cupola could be seen in the distance. It had been another miserable day, a cold wind sweeping in from the north and the rain still steadily falling. The men, and the ground on which they tried to snatch a few hours of fitful sleep, were still thoroughly saturated with water. Some of the men of the 19th Ohio, "having lost their blankets

and knapsacks, suffered terribly from the cold," wrote one soldier.

That night General Rosecrans issued a general order, trying to inspire the men for the expected battle the next morning. Rhetorically, it soared with the sort of high-flown appeal to valor that would have been better suited to the less jaded men of an earlier stage of the war.

Soldiers, the eyes of the whole nation are upon you, the very fate of the nation may be said to hang on the issue of this day's battle. Be true, then, to yourselves, true to your own manly character and soldierly reputation, true to the love of your dear ones at home, whose prayers ascend to God this day for your success.

Be cool! I need not ask you to be brave. Keep ranks. Do not throw away your fire. Fire slowly, deliberately; above all, fire low, and be always sure of your aim. Close steadily in upon the enemy, and, when you get within charging distance, rush on him with bayonet. Do this, and victory will certainly be yours.

There was no doubt that men who had been through what these men had been through would do their duty, out of sheer habit if nothing else. But there was another sentiment now emerging that some of the keener observers among the officers and men had noted over the past few days. It was a sentiment that allowed Reb and Yank to see themselves as enemies, to be sure, but enemies bound by a remarkably common fate. Both had been used cruelly by the war; both had grown doubtful and weary of the justifications they had once embraced for the fight; both had come to see themselves as hapless victims of a slightly mad world. They were enemies, to be sure, but the fire was already going out of the hatred.

A strange thing had happened a few days earlier, on the night of Sunday, December 28, that foreshadowed this change in the air. That day the two armies had maneuvered into a position that led Rosecrans to believe there was a very good chance the general battle would commence the next day. As dark fell and a Sunday stillness spread over the lines, the pickets on both sides of a creek that separated a Union and a Confederate unit had spontaneously emerged from the woods and, by cautious mutual consent, laid down their weapons and walked to the edge of the

creek for a chat. They spoke not as enemies riven by hate, but as rather ordinary men in the same business who had chanced to meet on the road and stopped to trade shop talk. Captain Thomas Wright of the 8th Kentucky jotted down one such exchange he overheard:

Rebel: "What command does you-ens belong to?"

Federal: "The Third Brigade."

Rebel: "Who commands that ar brigade?"

Federal: "Colonel Matthews. What is your command?"

Rebel: "We ar Wheeler's; an' I believe you-ens are the fellers we fit at Dobbins' Ferry."

Federal: "You bet we are! What did you think of us?"

Rebel: "Darned good marksmen; but whar yer fellers tryin' to go ter?"

Federal: "To Murfreesboro."

Rebel: "Well, you-ens'll find that are a mighty bloody job, sho."

Then the pickets had exchanged newspapers, quietly picked up their arms, and returned to their posts.

❧

There was much, of course, that bound the Northern and Southern soldier together. As different as North and South were socially, economically, religiously, and educationally in America's first century, they were still all Americans. They shared a common culture—a language, poetry, music, and core set of beliefs that were already distinctly American. The war, even as it tore the nation apart, had paradoxically brought the men who fought it together through their shared experience. Soldiers, Northern and Southern, had traveled beyond the bounds of their small hometowns, had been places most only dreamed of, had shared the terrible trials of combat, had seen the horrors of the dead and wounded on the battlefield. They not unsurprisingly felt they often had more in common with their counterparts in the opposing army than they did with their martinet generals or the blustering politicians and civilians who directed the war.

Music was in many ways the most universal part of American culture in the mid-nineteenth century. Songs traveled with uncanny speed across the nation, spread by minstrel shows, and published sheet music, or just from one person to another by word of mouth. A

distinctive American style, a blend of folk tunes from England and Scotland, gospel songs, minstrel tunes, and African-American spirituals, was embraced from New York to California, Maine to Georgia.

Music was also an inseparable part of the life of the soldier. "I don't believe we can have an army without music," remarked Robert E. Lee at one point in the war. Every morning the camps would rise to the familiar sound of reveille from the fife and drums, and every night "tattoo" sounded the final call to extinguish lanterns. But more important, every regiment had—or wanted to have—its own brass band. The bands were a source of huge pride, a vital boost to morale. While stationed at Nashville, the 21st Ohio had so chafed at not having its own band that it had gotten up a subscription among the men and raised an astonishing nine hundred dollars to buy a fine set of silver band instruments.

Composers responded to the coming of war with a flood of patriotic and sentimental songs, and many quickly became staples of the regimental bands' repertories. Some especially catchy tunes were sometimes adopted by both sides: "Battle Cry of Freedom" became a favorite of both the Union and the Confederate armies. The alternate words of the Northern and Southern versions were remarkable testimony to the common bonds that tied the two warring sides together. The Northern version was written in the summer of 1862 by George F. Root, one of the North's leading composers of Civil War anthems. A Southern version followed from composer H. L. Schreiner and lyricist W. H. Barnes. The words differed, but both asserted the claim to the mantle of the Revolution and the cause of freedom.

Union version: We will welcome to our numbers the loyal, true and brave,
Confederate version: They have laid down their lives on the bloody battlefield.

Shouting the battle cry of Freedom,
Shout, shout the battle cry of Freedom;

And although he may be poor, not a man shall be a slave,
Their motto is resistance, to tyrants we'll not yield!

Shouting the battle cry of Freedom.
Shout, shout the battle cry of Freedom.

The Union forever, Hurrah boys, Hurrah! Down with the
    traitor, up with the star;
Our Dixie forever, she's never at a loss. Down with the eagle, up with
    the cross.

While we rally 'round the flag, boys, rally once again,
We'll rally 'round the bonnie flag, we'll rally once again.

Shouting the battle cry of Freedom.
Shout, shout the battle cry of Freedom.

⁂

The battle lines that Rosecrans's men formed on the
afternoon of December 30 began along Stones River at
a ford a few miles downstream from Murfreesboro.
They crossed the Nashville Pike and the railroad along
a small, straight country road called McFadden's Lane,
which ran almost due north-south, separating a cedar
brake on the Nashville side from a cotton field on the
Murfreesboro side, and then continued roughly two
miles to the southwest through more cedar brakes and
farm fields. In many spots the Confederates had
drawn up only a few hundreds yards away.

    The atmosphere up and down the line was one of
"anxious suspense," recalled James Barnes of the 86th

Indiana. Trying to keep their rifles shielded from the constantly falling rain, they stood and waited, not knowing what to expect, or when. "The orders were to be ready at a moment's notice. The lines were forming. Batteries were being placed into position. Dark columns stood noiseless in the rain. Hospitals were established in the rear, and the musicians and other noncombatants were detailed to bear the stretchers and attend the ambulances. Medical stores were unpacked and countless rolls of bandages placed at hand for use. Provision trains were brought up and rations issued."

Rain dripped off the dark cedars and as night fell the woods and the dead cotton stalks took on a fantastic, eerie appearance. The cedars grew so dense in places that their branches dragged along the ground and touched from one tree to the next. In the fields, tufts of unpicked cotton clung to the stalks, specks of white amid the brown sodden twilight.

Things were every bit as unpleasant and tense on the Confederate lines. "When nightfall came we were in a lane with rail fences on each side, about four hundred yards from the main line of the enemy," recalled P. R. Jones of the 10th Texas:

The Eve of
Battle

Stones
River

Nashville Pike

To
Nashville

Ford

McFadden's
Lane

Round
Forest

Confederate
lines

Nashville & Chattanooga R.R.

Stones

River

Union
lines

Murfreesboro

0   Mile

N

Orders were to speak only in a whisper, as the enemy's pickets were not more than one hundred yards in front, the plan of battle being to take them by surprise next morning. We took down one of the lines of fence and spread the rails out over the ground next to the opposing string, which was left for breastworks. On the rails we passed the night without fires, most of the men sitting down watching the camp fires of the enemy some four hundred yards away, on an elevation.

We passed a most disagreeable night, having been on the battlefield all of the night before and at times pelted with heavy showers. I fortunately had a good wool blanket that I had brought from home, one of the old-fashioned kind, with a hole in the middle large enough for a man's head. I stuck my head through, pulled my hat down, took my loaded gun under the blanket, and thought of what would take place to-morrow.

Just before tattoo, in an effort to lift the air of gloom and apprehension, one of the Union regimental bands struck up a serenade. The familiar notes of "Yankee Doodle" filled the heavy and still night.

Just as the final chord died away, there came in the

distance an answering chorus from the Confederate lines, one of the Southern bands swinging into the equally familiar "Dixie." Then another Confederate band took up "The Bonnie Blue Flag":

We are a band of brothers and native to the soil,
Fighting for Liberty with treasure, blood, and toil;
And when our rights were threaten'd the cry rose near and far,
Hurrah for the Bonnie Blue Flag that bears a Single Star!

A Union regiment came charging back with "Hail, Columbia," like "Yankee Doodle," another song from the Revolution that the North had adopted as an anthem of its new fight in the Civil War:

Hail Columbia, happy land!
Hail, ye heroes, heav'n-born band,
Who fought and bled in freedom's cause,
And when the storm of war was gone
Enjoy'd the peace your valor won.
Let independence be our boast,
Ever mindful what it cost;
Ever grateful for the prize,
Let its altar reach the skies.

And then there occurred what many of the soldiers who were present would later remember as perhaps the strangest incident of the entire war.

Whether it was the lingering spirit of Christmas and nostalgic memories of home, or whether it was the feeling of shared destiny of the men who found themselves preparing to kill one another in the morn, or whether—most likely of all—it was a combination of the two, one of the bands struck up the sentimental air, "Home! Sweet Home!"

"The night before the battle an incident took place such as history seldom records," wrote Samuel Seay of the 1st Tennessee. "The opposing lines were so near to each other as to be within easy bugle-call. Just before 'tattoo,' the military bands on each side began their evening music. The still winter night carried their strains to a great distance. At every pause on our side, far away could be heard the military bands of the other.

"Finally one of them struck up 'Home! Sweet Home!' As if by common consent, all other airs ceased, and the bands of both armies, far as the ear could reach, joined in the refrain."

"Immediately a Confederate band caught up the

strain," recalled another Tennessee soldier of the incident, "then one after another until all the bands of each army were playing 'Home! Sweet Home!'"

Soon the men of both sides, North and South, were all raising their voices to sing the familiar words together:

> 'Mid pleasures and Palaces though we may roam,
> Be it ever so humble, there's no place like home!
> A charm from the skies seems to hallow us there,
> Which seek through the world, is ne'er met with
>   elsewhere.
> Home! Home, sweet sweet Home!
>
> To thee, I'll return overburdened with care,
> The heart's dearest solace will smile on me there.
> No more from that cottage again will I roam.
> Be it ever so humble, there's no place like home.
> Home! Home, sweet sweet Home!

And then the final, bittersweet line caught in the throats of the men who knew they shared a common fate—of very likely never returning to their homes again:

There's no place like home…
There's no-o place…like home!

"And after our bands had ceased playing," recalled the Tennessee soldier, "we could hear the sweet refrain as it died away on the cool frosty air on the Federal side." And so to a fitful and troubled sleep.

5

THE RIVER RAN RED

Thomas Long, a soldier of the 18th U.S. Regulars, was awoken early the following morning by a disturbing dream. In his dream he had seen the battle begin, and he himself was the first man in the regiment to fall, killed before he could ever fire his own gun.

As dawn came he confided his premonition to a fellow soldier, Robert Kennedy. "Bob," he said, "this is the last time I shall see the sunrise."

Kennedy sought out the company captain and informed him of Long's strange presentiment, and the officer came at once.

"Long, do you think you will be shot today?" the captain asked.

"Yes, Captain, I'll never fire my gun."

"Long, if you think that, fall out and go to the hospital."

"No, Captain," Long replied. "I'll die like a man, right with the company."

Another man who arose determined to show no fear and do his duty in spite of a premonition of doom was Rosecrans's aide, Colonel Julius P. Garesché. A strange and mystically devout veteran officer of the regular army, Garesché was a close friend of Rosecrans's and had been instrumental in converting him to Catholicism. Garesché combined his army duties with work for a Catholic lay order dedicated to relieving the suffering of the poor. He also immersed himself in the teachings of various Catholic mystics who believed that life was full of omens and portents to those who looked for them.

Garesché had turned down a major general's commission after Fort Sumter, insisting he would earn his promotion on the battlefield. But he did not expect to live to see that moment. There had been many signs, he insisted, that his days on earth were numbered. Once he had narrowly escaped death when the rising flood waters of the Missouri had swept away the cabin

in which he was sleeping. In Louisville, he was almost struck by a train. His brother, a Catholic priest who shared his mystical inclinations, interpreted these events as omens of impending doom. And then while assigned to army headquarters in Washington, Garesché had, while walking on the street with an acquaintance one day, grown angry and profane in talking of his many Southern relatives who had joined the Confederate side. The normally devout Garesché damned them all to a living hell. Then, shocked that he had so forgotten himself as to commit such a sin as cursing in such a manner, he confessed to his brother—who had told him that this too was a portent of his coming death. Indeed, his brother told him, he would die in his very first battle. No one since had been able to convince him otherwise.

❧

Several times during the night of December 30 the winter stillness had been disturbed by what, to a few unsleeping officers on the Union right, sounded like the rumble of gun carriages and the stealthy tramp of moving men. At two A.M. a brigade commander finally sought out his division commander, Brigadier

General Phil Sheridan, and woke him up to tell him what he heard. The two generals cautiously walked across an open field and into the thick cedar brake where the Union picket line was strung out. Even in daylight it was impossible to see more than fifty yards through the dense branches; by night it was like peering into a well. But the sounds coming through the wood were unmistakable. Convinced and disturbed, Sheridan returned to his horse and rode at once to awaken the commander of the army's Right Wing, Major General Alexander McDowell McCook.

The Right Wing commander was a West Point graduate, a veteran of the Indian wars in the West, an experienced tactical instructor, but he was also, as a newspaper reporter once described him, a sort of "overgrown schoolboy" who loved being the center of attention. "General McCook prides himself on being General McCook," cracked one soldier who had served under him. McCook airily waved away Sheridan's concerns. Rosecrans had ordered an attack on the Confederate right for first thing in the morning. That would put an end to whatever the Rebels might be trying to do with their creeping around in the night.

Still uneasy, Sheridan determined to do what he

could to at least ensure his division was ready. Walking along the line himself, on foot and unattended, he quietly found the majors of each of his regiments and passed on his order to have the men assemble, making as little noise as possible. By four in the morning all were under arms, the artillerymen ready at their cannons.

But the other divisions on the Union right continued their uneasy slumbers undisturbed by any orders to stand to. As day broke men straggled up and began to build fires and make coffee. "The comfort of warming chilled fingers and toes and drinking a grateful cup of coffee outweighed for the moment any consideration of danger," recalled Sergeant Major Lyman Widney of the 34th Illinois. Their comfort was not to last more than a few minutes. Widney vividly described what happened next:

I leisurely wandered out into the field towards the picket line, where a company of our regiment was stationed to watch the enemy. Before reaching them I saw one running towards me, and as he passed he exclaimed, "They're coming," and continued on to the regiment to give the alarm. As all was so quiet, not a

shot having been fired, I felt decidedly skeptical and walked still further out until the enemy's breast-works were in view. And there, sure enough, a succession of long lines of Gray were swarming over and sweeping towards us but not yet within gun-shot range.

I started back in a hurry to rejoin the regiment and met it, 350 men marching into an open field to meet 20,000. Our regiment had advanced about 100 yards when our pickets fired into the approaching columns of the enemy.

Our weak challenge was answered with a volley from one of the advancing regiments. . . . Our only salvation was to lie flat as possible on the ground, for the air fairly seethed with the zip of bullets and grape shot over our heads. It reminded me of the passage of a swarm of bees.

The Confederate army had had the same plan as Rosecrans, to attack the enemy right. And the Southerners had beaten him to the punch. Most of the Union right was caught as completely by surprise as Widney's regiment had been. "I noticed one of their dead some two hundred yards to the rear who had

been killed still holding firmly to his pot of coffee," noted J. A. Templeton of the 10th Texas Cavalry.

Only when the Confederates had actually smashed into the Union lines did they let out the Rebel yell. One Union soldier who witnessed the onslaught said that it looked like the entire Confederate army bursting out of the woods.

They struck with the force of a sledgehammer against tissue paper. It was "an assault which no troops in the world could have withstood," said a Union soldier in one of the regiments that absorbed the first blow. "We raised a whoop and a yell, and swooped down on those Yankees like a whirl-a-gust of woodpeckers in a hail storm," said one of the Confederates who saw action that morning. "Every man's gun was loaded, and they marched upon the blazing crest in solid file, and when they did fire there was a sudden lull in the storm of battle, because the Yankees were nearly all killed. I cannot remember ever seeing more dead men and horses and captured cannon, all jumbled together, than that scene of blood and carnage. The ground was literally covered with blue coats dead; and, if I remember correctly, there were eighty dead horses."

The entire Union right began to collapse. "Our comrades were falling as wheat falls before the cradling machines at harvest time," said J. H. Haynie of the 19th Illinois. "We could hear the hoarse shriek of shell . . . the impact of solid shot, the 'chug' when human forms were hit hard. Cannon balls cut down trees around and over us, which falling crushed living and dead alike." The collapse of the front lines started a contagious panic that quickly spread.

It soon threatened to become what many of the men and officers who witnessed it feared would be one of the worst disgraces in the history of the United States army as the demoralized troops began to flee to the rear, shouting, "All is lost!" Henry Castle, one of the Union soldiers who watched the pell-mell flight, said, "If there was anything more disgraceful at Bull Run than the scenes I witnessed in those cedars, I have not seen it described. All around us, and often breaking through us, was a yelling mob; officers weeping or swearing; soldiers demoralized and shivering."

"It is impossible to describe the scene adequately," wrote Henry V. Freeman, another who had what he called the misfortune to witness "the rear of a par-

tially defeated army." But the impressions of chaos, panic, and tarnished honor had remained vivid—and painful—years later when Freeman set down his recollections:

> Cannon and caissons, and remnants of batteries, the horses of which had been killed, were being hurriedly dragged off by hand. There were men retiring with guns, and men without guns; men limping, others holding up blood-stained arms and hands; men carrying off wounded comrades; and faces blackened with powder, and in some cases stained with blood. Two or three riderless horses dashed out of the woods which still partly hid the combat, for a distance, and stopped and stared back at the tumult. Over all rose, near at hand or more faintly from the distance, the yells of the rebel victors, answered occasionally by a cheer of defiance. . . . Among the men falling back there were some crying and some cursing. A man of Company K of the 74th Illinois . . . came up and said that a large part of the regiment had been killed or captured. He seemed to have some doubts whether anybody but himself had escaped.

The panicked retreat was halted only when the colonel of the 9th Michigan, which was acting as the provost guard of the Center Wing—the Union army's military police, in effect—decided to take matters into his own hands. He peremptorily ordered the entire regiment into line of battle across the Nashville Pike, its flanks extended as wide as possible. "Cavalry, artillery, infantry, sutlers, and camp followers came rushing with the force of a cyclone," said the colonel, "and the 9th Michigan was ordered to fix bayonets and charge upon this panic-stricken mass."

❧

Yet if panic was contagious, courage was too. And examples of spectacular courage on both sides of the fighting began to work an effect, tentatively at first, then more confidently.

Even in the midst of the initial collapse of the Federal lines, small acts of individual courage had inspired the men. Inspecting the deteriorating situation, Dr. Solon Marks, the chief medical officer of one of the Right Wing divisions, saw that a Union field hospital was about to be overrun. Marks called for volunteers among the surgeons at the hospital to remain

behind and tend to their patients. No one spoke up. Marks then dismounted from his horse and announced that the other surgeons could do as they wished, but he would stay right there and do his duty to the wounded men. "To their credit," Marks later wrote, "every surgeon returned to his duty and stood bravely to his post during the trying ordeal which followed. In a few minutes our troops had fallen back past our position." The surgeons remained prisoners of the Rebels, continuing, in the days that followed, to tend to the terrible wounds suffered by the men of their side.

On the Confederate side, the willingness of officers to share the risks of the common soldier had for the moment swept aside the days and weeks of bitterness that had infected the ranks. An astonishing act of courage by one South Carolina officer, Lieutenant C. Carrol White, became an instant legend throughout the Army of Tennessee. White's company had been deployed as skirmishers when a Union cavalry squadron suddenly swept in from the flank, taking White and a few other men prisoner. White at once bellowed out to the rest of his men, who had so far escaped capture, "Company A! Rally on the right!

Don't mind us—commence firing!" White and the other captured men dropped to the ground just as a volley from Company A crashed all around them into the Union cavalrymen. In a flash, White and the other South Carolinians were on their feet, pulling the Yankees who had escaped the hail of bullets out of their saddles. Within a few minutes the role of captive and captor had been reversed, and it was the Union cavalrymen who were prisoners.

At one point when the Confederate advance threatened to falter, division commander Major General B. Franklin Cheatham—who had a reputation as the most profane man in the Confederate army—suddenly appeared among the men. "Give 'em hell! Give 'em hell!" he shouted. "Come on boys and follow me!" And the general had then proceeded to lead the charge himself.

One soldier, wounded in the arm, was so astonished at the spectacle of a two-star general personally rushing an enemy artillery position that he dragged himself up, saying, "Well, General, if you are determined to die, I'll die with you." And so Cheatham had charged on, all the while shouting to his men, "Give 'em hell! Give 'em hell!"

Nearby while this was going on was Lieutenant General Leonidas Polk, his division commander—and the former Episcopal bishop of Louisiana. Polk was at a loss for a second. Then he joined in with "Give them what General Cheatham says, boys! Give them what General Cheatham says!"

Throughout the morning the Union right continued to buckle, swinging like a hinge back to the line of the Nashville Pike. At the pivot of the hinge was a small, unassuming bit of wood known locally as Round Forest, which lay just on the other side of the Pike, astride the railroad line. It would soon be known by another name: "Hell's Half Acre."

It was hard to say precisely what put the heart back into the demoralized Union men. Rosecrans's quick decision to cancel his own attack and shift units from the left and center to support the new defensive line along the vital Nashville Pike certainly helped. "The crisis seemed to rouse his every energy," recalled Freeman. Rosecrans was "the embodiment of courage, coolness and determination." "This battle must be won," he kept saying over and over. Riding up to the position on his army's vulnerable left flank along Stones River, Rosecrans demanded to know who commanded the brigade. A colonel stepped forward.

"Will you hold this ford?" Rosecrans asked.

"I will try, sir," the colonel answered.

"Will you hold this ford?" Rosecrans demanded again.

"I will die right here."

"Will you hold this ford?" a third time.

The colonel finally got the message. "Yes, sir," he replied.

"That will do," said Rosecrans, as he turned his horse and galloped off to another position.

It also helped that the very swiftness of the Confederate success had, willy-nilly, pushed back the Union artillery and so allowed the Union commanders to concentrate an awesome line of guns along the Pike. The advance through the thick, almost impenetrable cedars had meanwhile made it impossible for the Rebels to get their guns up to challenge them.

And yet there was something more. Some of the unsurpassed valor of the Rebels themselves had begun to rub off on their foes that morning. At one point it had been almost comical. A Confederate soldier, taken prisoner in an early skirmish, had

watched in disgust as the panicked Federals around him had broken and run before the advancing Rebels. Unable to contain himself he began shouting, "What yer running fer? Why don't yer stand and fight like men!" He had kept going in that vein, hotter and hotter, until a fellow Confederate prisoner interrupted him, "For God's sake, Joe, don't try to rally the Yankees. Keep 'em on the run!"

It was at Hell's Half Acre where courage on both sides joined in a crescendo of mutual valor. It was now clear to each side that this was the climax of the battle, the angle in the Union line at Round Forest, the crucial fulcrum of the Union position. If it fell, the Union army would lose its grip on the Pike and be cut off. After that it would just be a matter of picking up the pieces.

Charging a line of artillery was not as one-sided a venture as it might sound. The effective range of a cannon's canister shot, about three hundred yards, was no greater than a rifled musket's. If the flank of a line of artillery could be turned, the whole line was vulnerable: the guns could hardly turn and fire along their flanks without cannoning their own men up and down the line. And if the artillery horses were

picked off, the guns could be immobilized. It was not an impossible venture. It simply took courage of a kind that would seem to surpass all human understanding. So too was the courage required of artillerymen to stand to their guns, exposed completely without so much as a wooden rail to hide behind, while a line of infantry advanced.

Now as the crucial battle was joined, neither side wavered. The Union guns were lined up forty-five yards apart. At maximum effective range, the one-inch balls packed into a canister shot spread out about ninety yards. So if aimed well and fired briskly, the guns could lay down an impenetrable curtain of shot.

In midmorning the first wave of butternut-clad Rebels, a veteran brigade of Mississippians, burst from the wood beyond the Pike and started across the open cotton field that lay between them and the Union positions in the Round Forest. Fifty cannons opened with a staggering volley. Yet still the Mississippians kept coming—some of the soldiers pausing to pluck tufts of cotton from the field to stuff in their ears against the roar of the cannonade. Only when a third of them were cut down by musket fire from Union infantry did the attack collapse.

The noise of the battle was so great, recalled one artilleryman, that "birds sat in trees or on the ground, unable to fly, benumbed by the roar, rifle and cannon fire, shells bursting, men yelling, horses neighing, and wounded screaming made an awful crescendo." A former Murfreesboro slave would remember sixty years later how the tin pans in the cupboard had rattled and the house shook from the battle taking place miles away. "It sounded like the judgment," she said.

A little before noon a Tennessee brigade tried to take the Round Forest and drove to within yards of the Pike. But half of the 16th Tennessee was killed or wounded in the attempt; of the 425 men of the 8th Tennessee, an astonishing 306 were casualties. A final attempt just before sundown drove even farther, all the way into the forest, pushing the Union infantry back; then it too petered out.

As the sun set that New Year's Eve of 1862, nearly three thousand men lay dead, fifteen thousand wounded, across the cotton fields and cedar forests that had seen some of the bloodiest fighting of the entire terrible war. At one point during the fighting along Stones River, it was said that blood flowed so freely that the river literally ran red.

As night returned, so did the strange spirit of kinship between Yank and Reb that had manifested itself the night before.

There were no mingled choruses of "Home! Sweet Home!" tonight; even the bandsmen had fought, and they lay exhausted—or with the dead and wounded. "The frost, the dead and dying and the dark cedars among which we bivouacked were wild enough for a banquet of ghouls," wrote a Confederate brigadier general, William Preston, whose brigade lay just opposite the Round Forest that night. "I thought that night the longest Old Year out and New Year in that I ever watched for," Illinois soldier George Sinclair wrote his wife. "Although I had not slept three hours in the past three nights, I could not sleep a wink."

Some of the dead, wrote a soldier of the 73rd Illinois, "looked as though they had just fallen asleep—eyes closed, hands at their sides, and countenances unruffled. Others appeared as if their last moments had been spent in extreme pain—eyes open, and apparently ready to jump from their sockets; hands

grasping some portion of their garments and their features all distorted and changed."

Parties were cautiously sent from both Union and Confederate lines to aid the wounded and collect the dead, and quickly an informal truce took hold. "Hello, Johnny," came a tentative whisper from one side; "Hello, Yank," came the reply. "A mutual truce was granted," related Colonel William Blake of the 9th Indiana. "Soldiers of both sides, without arms, gathered their fallen comrades without interruption. The fierce acerbity of the deadly strife had given place to mutual expression of kindness and regard."

There were many spontaneous acts of sympathy, even solidarity. William McMurray of the 20th Tennessee told one story:

> We were placed on the picket line. . . . No one was in front of us but the Yankees and they were only about one hundred yards away. It was my duty as an officer to visit the different picket posts at intervals during the night. The night was cold and clear, the ground frozen to the depth of about one inch. While I was making my rounds, about one o'clock A.M., I heard a

halloahing and moaning some fifty yards in the rear of my picket line. I crept back upon a little rocky ravine until I was within a few yards of the noise and discovered a wounded soldier. I asked, "To what command do you belong?" He said, "Eighteenth Regulars," and that he was badly wounded and had been left here and was nearly frozen to death. He asked me to make a fire at his feet. I told him that I was a Confederate and on picket just in front of him, and by making a fire would draw the picket fire from the Yankees' pickets. He begged me pitifully, and as he was down in a ravine, I took the chances, and searched around among the rocks and got some cedar limbs and made him a fire and gave him some water, placed his head on his knapsack and made him as comfortable as possible. He said to me that the Eighteenth Regulars had fought some Tennessee Volunteers in this cedar brake that day, and they fought more like regulars than any volunteers he ever saw. He further said that they had killed and wounded nearly all of his regiment.

The poor fellow had bled and laid on the cold ground until life was nearly gone. When I left him I

told him if my line was not attacked or ordered away that I would come back before day and look after him. I went back in about two hours, but he had crossed over and was sleeping the soldier's sleep and I could do no more for him.

I returned to my duty, and next day as I was on the picket line for a while near this spot I counted seventeen minie balls in one cedar tree not over twelve inches in diameter, and twenty-two dead Federals within fifty feet of this tree.

Many a wounded soldier was given a sip from a canteen by men who had sought to kill him earlier in the day. "We took just the same care of the rebel wounded that we did of our own men," wrote Charles Doolittle, one Union soldier. "Many a one of them said we were different from what they had supposed."

The Illinois soldier Henry V. Freeman came upon a dying Confederate who begged that he would move him to a safer spot. "One of his legs had been mangled by a shell. He was carefully picked up on a blanket and, as tenderly as possible, carried a little to the rear, and given a drink of water from a canteen. He was exceedingly grateful, and requested, in case he died, that his mother, who he said lived in Alabama, might be written to." Freeman promised to carry out the man's wishes.

Later that night, ordered out on picket duty at midnight, Freeman came across "two severely wounded Confederates, for whom nothing could be done more than to supply water from my canteen to allay their thirst. One of them seemed very grateful. Both were dead when the morning of the new year, 1863, at length dawned. In the still watches of the night their sufferings had ended, before either of them could receive a surgeon's care. In the morning some kindly hand covered their faces with their hats and spread blankets over the poor remains of all that was mortal."

One of the most extraordinary acts of tribute to the fallen enemy that night was the respect paid to a Union colonel in Sheridan's division who had coura- geously attempted to hold the line against the Con- federate attack that morning. "A peculiar incident occurred in this fight in the cedar brake, the likes of which tends to soften the horrors of war, and strongly illustrates the respect that the true soldier has

for bravery and gallantry, even if exhibited by an enemy," Frank H. Smith of the 24th Tennessee wrote. He continued:

Colonel George V. Roberts of the 42nd Illinois was in command of the 3rd Brigade, which, with other troops under the command of Gen. Phil H. Sheridan, had been routed. Colonel Roberts tried in vain to stop the break in the Federal ranks caused by the charge of the Tennessee troops, and made effort after effort to reform and restore the broken lines. He was everywhere conspicuous for his bravery and daring, and about eleven o'clock he fell, killed by a minie ball.

Little wonder it is then that the Confederates gave him a soldier's funeral. After the lull in the fight, his late enemies dug a grave among the rocks and cedars. Major Luke W. Finlay wrapped him in his own military cloak and read the impressive service of the dead over his remains; the military salute was fired; "taps" sounded by the bugler.

All seemed over, but the private soldiers, especially of the 11th Tennessee, wanted to show their respect. So they brought a large smooth stone and placed it on Colonel Roberts's grave, and on this stone they

had laboriously scratched and chipped an inscription with a bayonet.

❧

Another funeral that took place in the frozen night was that of Colonel Julius Garesché. His prophesy of his own death had proved all too true. While riding alongside General Rosecrans late in the day toward the Round Forest, he had been struck by a cannon-ball and killed instantly. Rosecrans, who narrowly missed being killed himself, was bespattered with the blood of his friend and aide. "We cannot help it, brave men die in battle," muttered the general, and rode on. That night Garesché's friend Colonel William B. Hazen, who had commanded the brigade that had seen the worst fighting at the Round Forest, went out to search along the railroad tracks for Garesché's body. When he found it, he solemnly removed the West Point ring from the dead hand, picked up the copy of *The Imitation of Christ*, the book by the fifteenth century German mystic and monk Thomas à Kempis that Garesché always carried with him, and sent a squad to carry away the body. By the light of a

lantern, the soldiers dug a temporary grave for the fallen officer.

Thomas Long, the other Union soldier who had foreseen his own death, was laid to rest that night too. After he had told his captain that morning he would die like a man with the rest, his company had marched a quarter of a mile down the Pike and taken up a position by the roadside, lying on the ground. Five minutes later a minié ball plowed right through the right arm of the man next to him and struck him in the eye. He rolled over, recalled his friend Robert Kennedy, and never spoke another word.

6

NEW YEAR'S 1863

'A happy New Year to you,' said my comrade to me as we awoke from our slumbers this morning," recalled William Woodcock, the Union soldier in the 9th Kentucky who, a week before, had recorded in his diary the failed attempt to get a Christmas party going in his company. "But the occasional crash of the skirmishers' muskets that could be heard in front seemed to promise anything else than to verify his wish. . . . The morning opened bright and clear and the sun rose in all the beauty and majesty as if in derision," Woodcock continued—derision of the thousand of mangled bodies that lay unburied.

Henry V. Freeman spoke for many a comrade's feelings that morning when he later described the sensation of having survived that first day of the Battle of Stones River:

Most of us, I suppose, were at one time in our experience as soldiers rather anxious to participate in a battle. Perhaps we were not quite willing that the war would end without our having had that experience. If I had cherished any such feeling, it disappeared after Stones River. The war could not end any too soon thereafter, provided it ended in the triumph of the Union cause. Although three long years of fighting were yet to come, I never afterwards went into an engagement without the feeling, common, I presume, to most soldiers, that I would have been very glad if the necessity could have been rightfully and honorably avoided. We learned to know just what battles meant, and that even though we ourselves should escape that final sacrifice which is the last of earth and which so many of our comrades bravely rendered, our hearts would always be sore for comrades killed or wounded, and for surviving friends, after every battle, of those "Whose part in all the pomp that fills/The

circuit of the summer hills/Is that their graves are green."

It is too much to say that soldiers had learned at Stones River to fight again, yet to do so without hating one another. But it was true that the terrible bloodletting of the day before had reaffirmed a determination, and forged a bond of mutual respect, both of which had been absent before. As New Year's Day wore slowly on, the skirmishing fire died away and the unofficial truce held. Wagons rumbled all day up the Pike carrying the Union wounded off to Nashville. Civilians from the area ventured cautiously and stoically out onto the battlefield searching the faces of the dead for relatives and friends. "I spent most of the day searching for my fallen brother, but all in vain," reported one civilian. "He sleeps among the unknown dead. I went home."

In Murfreesboro, the courthouse and churches were pressed into service as hospitals and morgues. A lady who came to Murfreesboro in search of her son described the chaotic scene: "On entering town what a sight met my eyes! Prisoners entering every street, ambulances bringing in the wounded, every place

crowded with the dying, the Federal General Sill lying dead in the courthouse. . . . The churches were full of wounded, where the doctors were amputating legs and arms."

In one yard, rows of dead Union soldiers awaited burial. "With arm in sling I strolled over the yard, where lay in long rows hundreds of Federal dead, with narrow aisles between where one might walk and read the name, company, regiment, and state of each," wrote a wounded Confederate soldier, Joseph Hutcherson of the 3rd Georgia Battalion. "Oftentimes the simple word 'unknown' was pinned upon the dead soldier's breast. On the outer edge of this yard a long ditch was being dug the size of a large grave, but of great length."

One of the Confederate wounded awaiting treatment at the Murfreesboro courthouse was Spencer Talley. He was the young captain who had borrowed his colonel's coat just a week before so he could dance at the Christmas ball in the very same room. The contrast seemed incredible. Where tables had held delicacies and punch bowls, surgeons now worked in blood-spattered aprons. Where officers and the ladies of Murfreesboro had danced, now the wounded, the dying, and the dead crowded the floor. The evergreen decorations that still hung about the walls and windows were the only reminder that it was indeed the same place.

As Talley lay waiting for the surgeons to attend to his wound, the body of an officer was carried in and placed on the floor nearby. To his astonishment, Talley saw it was his colonel, killed in battle, wearing the very same coat that Talley had worn to the ball. "When his body was brought to the hospital my heart was full of sorrow and regardless of my wound I secured a vessel of water and washed his blood-stained face and hands," wrote Talley of this strange coincidence. "The coat which I had worn a few nights before to the grand ball and festival was now spotted and saturated with his life's blood. I removed the stains from his coat as best I could with the cold water and a rag, combed his unkempt hair and whiskers and laid his body with many others in the courthouse."

Other strange coincidences took place amid the chaos of tending to the dead and wounded in the days that followed the battle. One incident provided another small—if slightly comic—affirmation of the

common bond that tied the soldiers of the opposing sides together in the aftermath of so terrible a battle.

The background of the story had actually begun two years earlier. J. E. Robuck, a Confederate soldier, had been a medical student in Philadelphia just before the war. The rising sectional tensions following Lincoln's election had led the Northern and Southern students to exchange first insults, and then blows. Robuck had had his share of scraps. The Northern students had then chosen one of their largest classmates to teach Robuck a lesson. Tom Brooks, the medical student chosen to "whip" Robuck, weighed two hundred pounds; Robuck declined to fight against such an unfair advantage, angrily insisting that it was a "cowardly act" to put forward a man he could not possibly fight on equal terms. "But his provocations were such that when he cursed me I struck him in the face," Robuck recalled, "so he soon knocked me down and held me. I was powerless in his hands. He tried to force me to acknowledge that I was whipped, but I declined to do so. He at length took a large pocketknife from his pocket and struck me just over my right eye with the end of it, inflicting a painful wound. At this juncture the boys pulled him off. When I rose to my feet Brooks asked me if I was whipped. I told him plainly that I was not, that I was only overpowered."

At Stones River, Robuck had fought with the 29th Mississippi, taking part in one desperate charge against Union artillery. He had come through unscathed, but many in his unit had not been so fortunate, and at about ten o'clock in the morning on New Year's Day, Robuck went to a Confederate field hospital to visit some of his wounded comrades. Several Union surgeons had been permitted to cross the line under a flag of truce to tend to their own wounded who had been taken prisoner. The surgeons worked side by side in the cramped hospital.

"Very soon I was attracted by an argument between an Irish Yankee soldier and a Federal surgeon," Robuck recalled. "The Irishman was pleading for, and begging the surgeon not to amputate his leg, or rather his foot, as it was the ankle bone that had been fractured. Under all the surrounding circumstances, a scene like that attracted little or no attention whatever, yet it caused me to look in that direction. And soon the surgeon had my entire attention. There was something strangely familiar about his features."

Then another Union surgeon approached the table to examine the patient and Robuck heard him say, "I fail to find the necessity for an amputation in this case, Brooks." It was indeed Brooks, his erstwhile tormentor. But, Robuck observed, he was not the man he had been:

He was not so robust, and I had noticed him take frequent drinks from a flask drawn from his coat pocket. While he had lost, I had gained, and weighed now one hundred and seventy-five pounds, in perfect health, and felt stout as a mule. I stepped in front of him and asked:

"Are you Doctor Brooks?"

Waving his hand and bowing, he replied: "I have the honor, sir."

"You also have the honor of having whipped me once in the city of Philadelphia, and now since we have met again I propose to renew the contest."

He eyed me a moment, in evident surprise, then asked bluntly, "Are you Robuck?" Bowing politely and waving my hand in mimicry of his own style, I replied, "I have the honor, sir."

He hastily placed his instruments on the table,

drew forth his flask, swallowed a draught of brandy, drew off and threw aside his coat, and rushed at me like a maniac. Being partially intoxicated, he was not strictly on his guard. So when he rushed at me, I knocked him down, and desiring to hold my advantage, I covered and held him down. And there I held Dr. Brooks and pounded him until he acknowledged that he was whipped. In the meantime his Irish patient had raised up on the table and kept calling out to me, "Give it to 'im good, Johnnie Reb! Kill 'im and save me leg! Maul 'im good!"

⚜

In the past when the armies of North and South had suffered losses like they suffered at Stones River, commanders had been quick to break off action. Bragg was convinced the Yankees would do the same again. He even cabled a victory telegram to Richmond. "The enemy has yielded his strong position and is falling back. We occupy the whole field and shall follow him. . . . God has granted us a happy New Year."

Hearing the sounds of the wagons rumbling up the Nashville Pike, Bragg in fact thought that Rosecrans

was already pulling out. Yet if the last lingering illusions of war had vanished now, so had the demoralization.

The Union troops had barely had food that day. Some received a few crackers, some a handful of parched corn, some a half pint of beans, some a quarter pint of flour, some a few ears of corn, some nothing at all. And yet they were ready to fight on. Colonel John Beatty of the 3rd Ohio felt the new optimism as he huddled by the campfire that night. "I draw closer to the camp-fire, and, pushing the brands together, take out my little Bible, and as I open it my eyes fall on the xci Psalm: 'I will say of the Lord, He is my refuge and my fortress, my God, in Him I will trust.'"

The pause on New Year's Day was not the shock of shattered and demoralized men, but an act of mutual respect for the experience they now shared. In fact, Rosecrans had already made the decision to stand. At midnight he had summoned a council of war to his headquarters, a small cabin on the Nashville Pike. One of his generals had cautiously let fall a suggestion of retreat. Major General George H. Thomas, commander of the Center Wing, by far the most competent of Rosecrans's subordinates, had been dozing. But he

started awake at the word "retreat," muttered, "This army does not retreat. I know no better place to die than right here," then fell promptly back to sleep.

Rosecrans settled the matter. "Gentlemen, we have come to fight and win this battle, and we shall do it. Our supplies may run short, but we will have our trains out again tomorrow. We will keep right on, and eat corn for a week, but we will win this battle. We can and will do it."

There had been another event on that New Year's Day that would change what men were fighting for. Though it had gone unremarked by most, and was far from universally welcomed at first, January 1, 1863, was the day that Lincoln's final Emancipation Proclamation went into force. Stones River marked the start of two years of nearly continuous fighting that now would not end until the nation was one and all men were equally free. And though they were destined to lose the war, the soldiers of the Confederacy found at Stones River renewed faith in the unsurpassed courage that would be their enduring trait throughout the war, and their enduring legacy to the nation.

The following day the fighting resumed. In one terrible half hour, eighteen hundred Confederates were

once again mowed down by Union artillery, this time along the ford of Stones River itself to the north of the Pike and the railroad. The next day Bragg pulled back to a defensive line behind the Duck River south of Murfreesboro.

It was not much of a victory for the North. In the end the Union side had 1,700 killed, 7,800 wounded and 3,700 taken prisoner or missing. In terms of the percentage of men lost, it was the most costly engagement of the entire war: 13,200 casualties out of an army of 41,400. The southerners had 1,300 dead, 7,900 wounded and 1,000 captured or missing.

But it was a victory nonetheless, for the North a desperately needed ray of hope at a crucial moment, especially in the war for public opinion in Europe. After some hesitation, while confused reports from the scene made their way across the ocean, the London newspapers began to report the battle as a critical Union success.

Shortly after the battle, one Union soldier wrote:

Before this battle took place, the outlook for our country was very dark and threatening. Our armies had gained no signal victories for many months, and

there was very great danger that some of the Nations of Europe would recognize the Southern Confederacy, and that it would be impossible for us to maintain our blockade. Had General Rosecrans' Army been defeated at the battle of Stones River . . . it would not only have prolonged the War, but would have greatly increased our danger of conflicts with foreign countries.

Lincoln sent his personal thanks. "God bless you, and all with you," he wrote Rosecrans. "Please tender to all, and accept for yourself, the nation's gratitude for your and their skill, endurance, and dauntless courage." Eight months later Lincoln reiterated the importance of the battle as a turning point of the war. "I can never forget, whilst I remember anything, that about the end of last year and the beginning of this, you gave us a hard-earned victory, which, had there been a defeat instead, the nation could scarcely have lived over."

❧✦❧

It was in this season of renewed faith that Henry Wadsworth Longfellow wrote a Christmas poem, later set to music, that remains a popular carol still sung to this day. These days, it is mostly only the first verse, or the first few, that are remembered:

I heard the bells on Christmas Day
Their old familiar carols play,
And wild and sweet
The words repeat
Of peace on earth, good-will to men!

And thought how, as the day had come,
The belfries of all Christendom
Had rolled along
The unbroken song
Of peace on earth, good-will to men!

Till, ringing, singing on its way,
The world revolved from night to day,
A voice, a chime
A chant sublime
Of peace on earth, good-will to men!

But there were four other verses that Longfellow had originally written, which are now largely

forgotten. They spoke directly to the events of the war that Christmas 1862 and of the renewal of faith in a time of terrible trial. The first of these verses evoked the cannons' roar now heard across the land: "And with the sound/The carols drowned/Of peace on earth, good-will to men!"

And then Longfellow continued:

> It was as if an earthquake rent
> The hearth-stones of a continent,
> And made forlorn
> The households born
> Of peace on earth, good-will to men!
>
> And in despair I bowed my head;
> "There is no peace on earth," I said;
> "For hate is strong,
> And mocks the song
> Of peace on earth, good-will to men!"

But then, the last verse brought a triumphant re-affirmation of the Christmas message. It was the message of universal peace, of God's love for mankind, and of simple, perhaps even childlike, hope:

Then pealed the bells more loud and deep:
"God is not dead; nor doth he sleep!
The Wrong shall fail,
The Right prevail,
With peace on earth, good-will to men!"

❧

On the first Sunday following the battle, January 4, 1863, Rosecrans attended Mass in a small cabin. "It was a beautiful morning," said one Union soldier who was there. "Dead soldiers and horses were still strewn over the fields, and burial parties were engaged at their solemn task. The General in command, his staff and guests, assembled in and around that cabin, while the holy rites were celebrated, and a short address delivered by our chaplain, from the text: 'In Ramah was there a voice heard, lamentation, and weeping, and great mourning, Rachel weeping for her children, and would not be comforted, because they were not.' Every heart was touched, and pent-up feelings of strong men who had striven in those scenes of battle sought relief in tears."

❧

The first steps toward commemorating the battlefield, steps that would play an important part in the final reconciliation of North and South that would follow the war, began almost immediately after the Battle of Stones River. Many of the dead had been hastily buried in rows of mass graves, their locations marked on "ghoul's maps" by the burial details so that they might later be properly reburied or sent home. The comrades of one Ohio soldier wrote a wrenching letter to the man's family giving instructions that they hoped would permit them to find his makeshift grave in case they should be able to make the journey down to Tennessee. "Allen's grave," they wrote, "is about one and a half miles northwest of this place. I think I would cross at the railroad bridge or above it. Go up the river about a mile and go one mile north. It is in a woods pasture a good many cedars, tall grass and timber about 100 yards east of the branch. About 300 yards west there is a fine frame house burnt, there is a chimney standing there with a large black oak tree standing almost in front of the farm. And all are marked by headboards. It could easily be found by asking citizens and Negroes in the neighborhood where the battle commenced."

The army paid for officers' remains to be transported home for burial, but the families of many enlisted men could not afford the expense. Colonel Hazen's men, who had fought so valiantly at the Round Forest, accordingly decided that the permanent resting place for their fallen comrades would be on this piece of Southern soil. They gathered the dead of their brigade close to the spot where they had died, placed each under a simple stone marker, and built a stone wall around the place. And later that year a large square stone monument was erected in the center of the enclosure, which stood on a slight rise in the small triangular sliver of ground between the Pike and the railroad. Engraved on the sides were simple words of tribute:

ERECTED 1863 UPON THE GROUND
WHERE THEY FELL.
BY THEIR COMRADES.

THE BLOOD OF ONE THIRD OF ITS SOLDIERS
TWICE SPILLED IN TENNESSEE
CRIMSONS THE BATTLE FLAG OF THE BRIGADE
AND INSPIRES TO GREATER DEEDS.

A more significant memorial began to take root immediately following the war. Under an act of Congress authorizing the establishment of national cemeteries for war dead, a Union chaplain was appointed to oversee the task of disinterring the dead who still lay haphazardly buried all over the Stones River battlefield and reburying them in a new ground that stood on a rise just north of Hazen's monument. It was close to where the line of Union guns had stood during the terrible scenes of bravery and carnage on the last day of 1862. The stony woods and fields were combed for graves and the daunting work got under way. And on eighteen once torn and scarred acres where the cannon had boomed and men had fallen in agony or death, there now appeared sixty-one hundred gravestones in orderly rows, amid a calm shade of overarching trees and green lawns.

A lone cannon remains amid the graves to mark where the Union artillery line stood. But it is less an appeal to awake the martial spirit than a reminder that it is the dead who are now in possession of the field where a war was once fought.

On the day that Stones River Military Park was formally dedicated, July 15, 1932, the American flag was

raised over the Union dead by Sam Mitchell, a former Confederate soldier.

❧❦❧

Christmas itself became part of the reconciliation that drew North and South back together in the years immediately following the end of the war. The nostalgic yearnings that had magnified Christmas in the hearts of soldiers so far from home had, after the war, been joined by a yearning for the promise of peace and well-being that Christmas held out to a war-torn nation.

It was natural for men who had suffered so heavily, and for families who had lost all, to seek some deeper meaning in their tragedy. Over time, the harsher truths about the war would inevitably become wrapped in a comforting and romantic haze. The heroic statues and monuments, depicting soldiers standing tall and proud and ever young and unscathed; the joint "Blue and Gray" reunions in which the former foes, on the anniversaries of great battles, embraced one another on the very fields where they had once slaughtered one another; the annual decoration of soldiers' graves neatly laid out in green and

serene cemeteries: all these contributed to a sentimental amnesia in which the worst of the war's horrors were forgotten. Walt Whitman, in a speech he prepared but in the end never gave, wrote the famous words that have been applied to wars ever since: "The real war will never get in the books."

And yet the urge of Americans to see in their late Civil War and return to peace not a triumph of one side over the other, but of both over a common affliction, was not mere moonshine or false sentiment. It arose from the common bonds of suffering that had been forged at Stones River and elsewhere among the ordinary men who came to know and honor their foes even as they fought and killed and died; it came from the slowly dawning awareness among the more reflective men of a reunited nation that, in that terrible mutual sacrifice, a destiny greater than either side had intended had been fulfilled. Lincoln had put his finger on it in his Second Inaugural Address—his last great speech, delivered just six weeks before his assassination as the end of the ordeal was in sight. "Neither party expected for the war the magnitude, or the duration which it has already attained," he acknowledged. "Each looked for an easier triumph, and a result

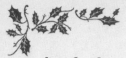

less fundamental and astounding. Both read the same Bible, and pray to the same God; and each invokes His aid against the other.... The prayers of both could not be answered; that of neither has been answered fully. The Almighty has His own purposes." That purpose, Lincoln suggested simply, was ridding America of the sin of slavery. Perhaps it was even God's will that "every drop of blood drawn with the lash shall be paid by another drawn with the sword." And so from the blood of North and South had come the redemption of the nation.

Then came the immortal words with which Lincoln concluded: "With malice toward none; with charity toward all . . . let us strive on to finish the work we are in; to bind up the nation's wounds; to care for him who shall have borne the battle, and for his widow, and his orphan—to do all which may achieve and cherish a just, and a lasting peace, among ourselves, and with all nations."

It was no coincidence that the simple story of Christmas now echoed so resonantly in the hearts of Americans. All of the new feelings about Christmas that had been slowly building in the decades before the Civil War burst into full bloom with the coming

of peace. The war's "dramatic backdrop, against which the silhouette of Christmas sharpened, fixed Christmas in the national imagination," writes the historian Penne Restad in *Christmas in America.* "Christmas held within it a rich preserve for grappling with issues of absence, discord, misunderstanding, forgiveness, and regeneration. It beckoned men and women past earthly travail into . . . a domestic haven that was neither particularly Northern or Southern."

The Civil War, in fact, made Christmas a truly American holiday in a way it had never entirely been before. Before the Civil War, Sarah Hale, the editor of *Godey's Lady's Book,* had been a stalwart advocate of Thanksgiving as *the* national holiday for Americans. But after the war she began to see Christmas as having a higher claim in the nation's heart. "Christmas," she wrote, "holds the celestial magnet of brotherhood that should draw all who enjoy its blessing into that feeling of National Union." In her December 1865 editorial, Hale listed "peace and goodwill to our family of States" as one of the season's Christmas gifts. "Should not the American people become, on this Christmas, like little children in their feelings of love and gratitude to our Heavenly Father, for his great

gifts of peace and good-will to our family of States?"
she asked.

Harper's Weekly struck the same theme in an elegy
that appeared in its Christmas issue of 1865, celebrating that first Christmas of the return of peace:

> The Christmas greeting of this year will be more ex-
> citing than for many a year past. For if all the clouds
> that lowered upon our house are not in the deep
> bosom of the ocean buried, the sun has fully pierced
> them, and the genial light of peace makes such a fes-
> tival as has long been unknown to us....
>
> Every American trusts the public sagacity and
> heroism as he never did before.... If we are prouder
> than ever before, it is legitimate pride. If we are more
> confident, it is justifiable faith. For if ever there were
> a true movement of the people it was the late war,
> and if ever a people moved steadily and nobly for-
> ward it was this people who did it.
>
> For the heroic dead, the flower of our youth
> which the fierce war withered, there will be a forever
> renewed tenderness of private remembrance and of
> public respect with every Christmas season. For the
> living who returned from the bitter field there will be

always at every season a Christmas welcome in all faithful hearts. For those who so long maintained the fight against the Union there will always be mingled feelings as the old domestic and religious feast returns. Yet among those feelings hate and vindictiveness have no share. The festival commemorates the birth of Him who died for all men, and thereby proclaimed and sealed their common humanity.

And if the Christmas light could show the late enemies... that peace is born only of good will to men, we should all gladly join hands from sea to sea and raise our voice in one vast millennial chorus, the jubilant thunder of which would break all political, moral, social, and mental chains in the world, "Glory to God in the highest, peace on earth, good will to men!"

By 1870 the United States Congress had established Christmas as a national holiday for the first time. A host of new traditions arose. Christmas trees, which even as they had slowly been growing in popularity in the years before the war had always been associated closely with the traditional German Christmas, quickly became a wholly American tradition,

embraced everywhere. Stores now filled each year with a cornucopia of Christmas ornaments for decorating trees—Santa Clauses, globes, flowers of colored glass, bright tin reflectors, clowns with caps and bells, storybook characters, even figures of George Washington. The popularity of sending Christmas cards soared. The years immediately after the war brought new Christmas songs from the pens of American writers and musicians: "O Little Town of Bethlehem" and "Away in a Manger," among many others. The tradition of caroling became hugely popular in towns and cities across the nation. Following the Civil War, huge crowds packed into a New York armory each December to join in a mass singing of Handel's *Messiah*.

The mass migration and social dislocation the war had left in its wake made a holiday tied to the timeless cornerstones of family and children all the more important to a restless and growing nation.

❧

It was in this first Christmas season after the war's end that a final poignant reminder of the shared trials of the men who fought at Stones River came wafting

back. Henry V. Freeman had never forgotten his promise to the dying Alabama soldier to write his mother and tell her of his fate on the battlefield. Freeman had written down her address and carried it with him until the end of the war: M. W. Wildy, Davis Creek Post Office, Fayette County, Alabama. And so when the fighting had ended, he wrote and told of the wounded soldier he had found lying next to a gun of a captured Confederate battery, and how the man had caught hold of Freeman's overcoat as he had passed and begged to be carried back to a safer and more comfortable spot. And how the Union men had tenderly lifted him up and given him a drink of water. And how they had promised to write his mother.

But whether the man's mother had moved or died, or whether the post office no longer existed, the letter had now come back, undeliverable.

❧❦❧

To those who had seen the face of battle, the Christmas of 1865 was one they would never forget. Nor would any subsequent Christmas ever seem quite the same as it had in the years before the war. In that first Christmas of peace, *Harper's* had printed a poem called

"By the Christmas Hearth" that captured the simple power of this so old yet newfound holiday for the men who had given so much, men who had learned to have faith in themselves—and goodwill toward their foes.

> … *We keep our Christmas, so unlike*
>   *The Christmas of a year ago,*
> *When in the camp at earliest dawn*
>   *The grimy-throated cannon woke*
> *Our slumbers…*
>
> *Ah! Then the smoke of battle hung*
>   *Its sulphrous cloud our land above,*
> *And bitter feud and hatred filled*
>   *Brave hearts that should have warmed with Love…*
>
> *So sweet it seems at home once more*
>   *To sit with those we hold most dear,*
> *And keep absence once again*
>   *To keep the Merry Christmas here.*

SOURCES

Books and Articles

Andrews, J. Cutler. *The North Reports the Civil War*. Pittsburgh: University of Pittsburgh Press, 1955.

The Battle of Stones River. Eastern Acorn Press, 1987.

Catton, Bruce. *This Hallowed Ground: The Story of the Union Side of the Civil War*. Garden City, New York: Doubleday, 1962.

Cozzens, Peter. *No Better Place to Die: The Battle of Stones River*. Urbana: University of Illinois Press, 1990.

——. *The Battle of Stones River*. National Parks Civil War Series. Eastern National, 1995.

Everson, Guy R., and Edward W. Simpson, eds. *"Far, Far From Home": The Wartime Letters of Dick and Tally Simpson, Third South Carolina Volunteers*. New York: Oxford University Press, 1994.

Foner, Eric. *Reconstruction: America's Unfinished Revolution, 1863–1877*. New York: Harper & Row, 1988.

Foote, Shelby. *The Civil War: A Narrative*. New York: Random House, 1974.

Freeman, Henry V. "Some Battle Recollections of Stone's River." *Military Essays and Recollections.* Papers read before the Commandery of the State of Illinois, Military Order of the Loyal Legion of the United States. Vol. 3. Chicago, 1891–.

Garrett, Jill Knight, and Marise P. Lightfoot. *The Civil War in Maury County, Tennessee.* Columbia, Tennessee, 1966.

Jones, J. B. *A Rebel War Clerk's Diary at the Confederate States Capital.* Philadelphia: Lippincott, 1866.

Jones, Shirley Farris. "Morgan's Wedding." Rutherford County Historical Society. Publication No. 34, 1994, pp. 1–21.

Lamers, William M. *The Edge of Glory: A Biography of General William S. Rosecrans, U.S.A.* New York: Harcourt, Brace, 1961.

Lawson, Samuel J., III. "The Role of Stone's River in the Early Exploration, Trade, and Settlement of Rutherford County, Tennessee." Rutherford County Historical Society. Publication No. 18, Winter 1982, pp. 89–137.

Logsdon, David R. *Eyewitnesses at the Battle of Stones River.* Nashville, Tennessee: Kettle Mills Press, 1989.

McDonough, James Lee. *Stones River—Bloody Winter in Tennessee.* Knoxville: University of Tennessee Press, 1980.

——. "The Last Day at Stones River—Experiences of a Yank and a Reb." *Tennessee Historical Quarterly* 40 (1981), pp. 3–12.

McMurray, William Josiah. *History of the Twentieth Regiment Volunteer Infantry, C.S.A.* Nashville, Tennessee: The Publication Committee, 1904.

McPherson, James M. *Battle Cry of Freedom.* New York: Oxford University Press, 1988.

Nissenbaum, Stephen. *The Battle for Christmas.* New York: Knopf, 1996.

Parkhurst, John G. *Recollections of Stone's River.* Detroit: Winn & Hammond, 1890.

Rawlings, Kevin. *We Were Marching on Christmas Day: A History and Chronicle of Christmas During the Civil War.* Baltimore: Toomey Press, 1996.

Restad, Penne L. *Christmas in America: A History.* New York: Oxford University Press, 1995.

Robuck, J. E. *My Own Personal Experience and Observation as a Soldier in the Confederate Army.* Reprint. Memphis, Tennessee: Burke's Book Store, 1986.

"A View of the Battlefield of Stones River." Rutherford County Historical Society. Publication No. 8, Winter 1977, pp. 75–80.

Womack, Bob. "The River Ran Red With Men's Blood." *Accent* (magazine of the *Daily News Journal,* Murfreesboro, Tennessee). December 26, 1976.

*Copies of Unpublished Letters and Diaries
at Stones River National Battlefield*

Azra Bartholomew, Jr.
Reuben Jones
Robert Kennedy
James S. McCarty
E. P. Norman
George B. Ridenour
Reuben Searcy
George G. Sinclair
William M. Woodcock

Unpublished Letters at the Center for Archival Collections,
Bowling Green State University

Alfred D. Searles

Unpublished Letters and Diaries of the
114th Ohio Volunteer Infantry

Elias D. Moore

Papers and Local History Publications at the
Albert Gore Research Center, Middle Tennessee State University

Community collection
Womack collection

American Christmas Classics

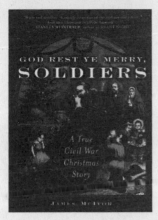

ISBN: 0-452-28769-3
Price: $12.00 / $15.00 CAN.

ISBN: 0-452-28367-1
Price: $14.00 / $20.00 CAN.

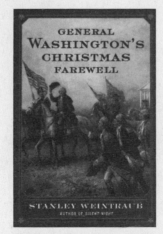

ISBN: 0-452-28532-1
Price: $14.00 / $20.00 CAN.

Available wherever books are sold.